Horary Examples

Traditional Horary Astrology By Example

By Fotini Christodoulou, Leah Cuperman, John Frawley, Marcos Monteiro
Molly Morrissey, and Kathryn Silvestre

Edited by Dave Menconi

Dedication

Dedicated to Clifford H. Low who was the inspiration for this book, although he scarcely knows it.

Written by Fotini Christodoulou, Leah Cuperman, John Frawley, Marcos Monteiro, Molly Morrissey, Kathryn Silvestre
Edited by Dave Menconi.

Acknowledgements

This book started with a lecture on Astrology by Clifford H. Low at PantheaCon. Mr. Low had such enthusiasm for Astrology that I wanted to learn more.

In the bibliography from his handout was the name of a book by John Frawley and I read it and then another. I had some questions for Mr. Frawley who very kindly answered them. Eventually I was studying horary avidly but I felt I needed more examples. I looked around and couldn't find many (*Warnock's Horary Casebook* being the lone example) so I asked Mr. Frawley if he would be interested in writing a book to fill this need. He encouraged me to assemble a book myself and suggested a few potential authors.

This book, then, is the product of a series of apparently random connections from PantheaCon to Mr. Low to Mr. Frawley to the other authors of the book. I would like to acknowledge all of them.

I would also like to acknowledge Kathryn Silvestre who did a lot of extra writing and editing on this book without complaint or extra compensation.

And, of course, all the authors whose long dedication and patience with their editor made this book a reality.

Finally, I'd like to thank my wife, Dorita Menconi, who is long suffering and very forgiving.

The charts in this book were created by Solar Fire software by Astrolabe, https://alabe.com/solargold.html

Table of Contents

Introduction

By Kathryn Silvestre

Horary is a branch of astrology that provides specific answers to specific questions by means of a horoscope. Before the modern era, horary was the mainstay of astrological practice in the western world; natal astrology was a practice reserved for the nobility.

Horary is the foundational branch within what is known as traditional astrology. Traditional astrology differs in significant ways from modern astrology, the stream most people are familiar with through sun-sign columns and popular websites. It's important to note, however, that both "traditional" and "modern" are very broad terms in themselves.

Most people curious about astrology today know little or nothing about horary. This book has been compiled to give the reader a collection of soundly judged horary charts to read and study, written by the astrologers who judged those charts. We hope that this collection of examples will give the reader ample opportunity to see how horary works and how useful it can be in addressing the huge variety of concerns that arise in daily life.

In order to best understand horary, one should be familiar with the philosophical principles upon which it rests. As these vary a great deal from modern worldviews, let's take a moment to articulate a few of them here:

We live in a created universe, where nothing is random and everything is interconnected and meaningful. That the universe is created means there is a Creator – God – and there are God's creatures – us. Of all the statements that can be made about astrology, this is probably the single most important.

The second most important statement is perhaps this: we are not in charge of things; God is. We exercise our free will within God's creation, which has an established order and workings.

There are two realms within creation: the time-bound realm, which we inhabit, and the eternal realm, which is beyond. In our realm, time flows by in a never-ending stream according to laws that do not vary. We move within time, bound by these same laws.

The realm of time is divided into planetary spheres, of which there are seven. These correspond with the seven heavenly bodies, beginning with Saturn and proceeding downward through Jupiter, Mars, the Sun, Venus, Mercury, and the Moon. These are the seven planets of our cosmos (although technically the Sun and the Moon are luminaries, not planets). Earth is not so much at the center of the cosmos as at the bottom. Above the sphere of Saturn is that of the fixed stars, and beyond that is the eternal realm, infinite and timeless.

Everything in the realm of time is made up of the same stuff, the common materials of creation. These materials are symbolized by these same seven planets: Saturn, Jupiter, Mars, the Sun, Venus, Mercury, and the Moon.

All things that share in essence move in accordance with each other. Saturn stuff moves along with Saturn, Jupiter stuff with Jupiter, and so on. Because we are made up of these same seven materials, as they move and change, so do we. This is what is meant by the familiar phrase "As above, so below." The planets and stars above us serve as a mirror of what is happening here on Earth. It is reflection, not causation.

Everything that was, is, and shall be, has already happened and exists in the eternal realm outside of time. Because we live in the time-bound realm, we experience time and life as linear. But in fact, our lives are already complete. To borrow an analogy from my teacher, John Frawley, the house is already built. We see only this room because it's where we are now in the stream of time. The very reason we can predict things using horary astrology is because the whole house is already built. Otherwise, how could we predict anything? We could not.

Horary is a snapshot, a still-frame, of the stream of time as it flows by. Studying a horary chart, we can see both what is happening now and what is ahead. Horary astrology gives accurate results that are verifiable. It works and can be seen to work. The examples in this book will show you just how precisely it works!

The astrologer judges a horary chart following a specific methodology. In brief, here is the method: Someone asks a question on a matter of importance to them. When the question reaches the ears or eyes of an astrologer with the knowledge to judge the chart, the question is born. To find the answer within the chart, the astrologer identifies which houses are involved, signifying the subject at hand, and then which planets rule those houses. Based on the condition of those planets and their relationship to other planets in the chart, we can see what is happening now and what is ahead within the context defined by the question.

Correct identification of the houses and planets for the question is the key to accurate judgment in horary. Sometimes this is easy, and sometimes it is not. Even experienced horary astrologers can make mistakes, and no astrologer is infallible.

Every horary chart can be judged. Statements and beliefs to the contrary – such as “considerations before judgment” – were written in order to give the astrologer a way out when he didn’t want to judge the question, or when judging it might put him in danger.

The marvel of horary is that we can see the workings of God’s universe through the chart. In the end it is a comfort to know that there is order in the world, and that God’s hand is guiding all of creation. Seeing this at work in a horary chart is an amazing thing. It changes you!

Please enjoy these fine examples of the marvelous art that is horary astrology.

Contests

Will Deirdre Be Sent Down?

John Frawley

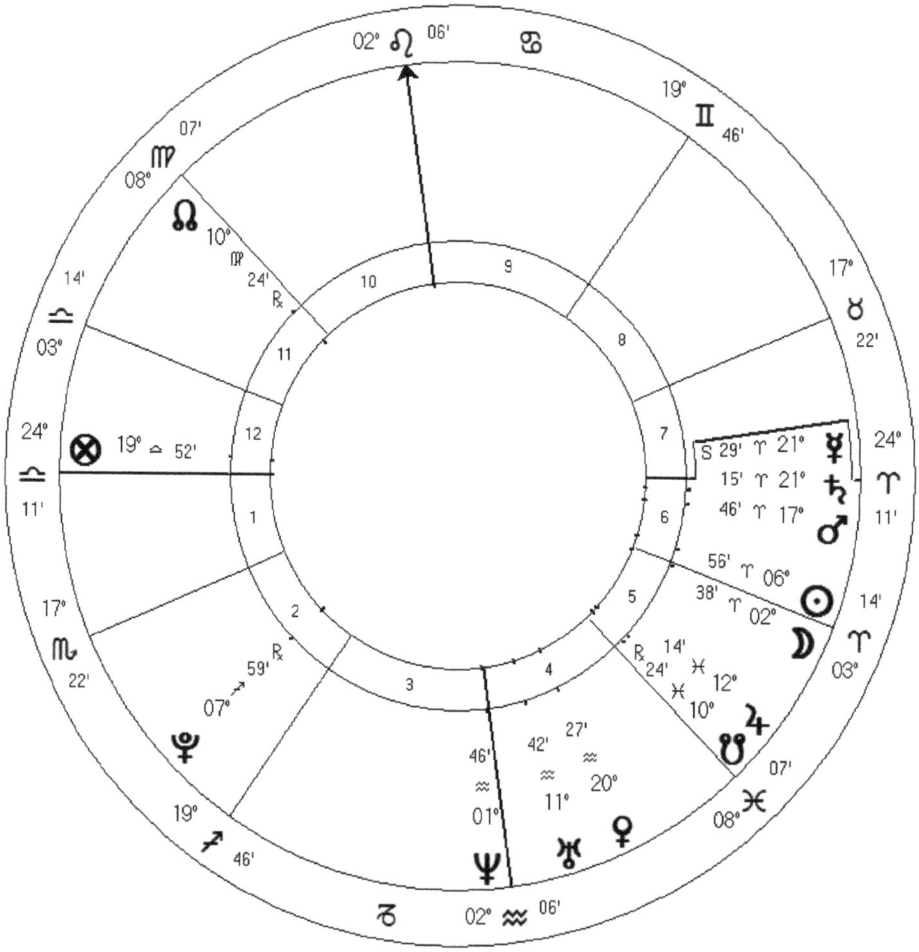

March 27, 1998, 7:58 P.M. | London, England | 24 Libra

To while away long evenings, William Lilly (see Glossary) would "in merriment" ask a servant to hide something and then cast a chart to find it. I have never developed his affection for lost object questions; my preferred horary merriment comes in predicting the story line in soap operas.

In *Coronation Street*, Deirdre was in the dock, facing charges of fraud after falling for a charming but unscrupulous con-man. As the foreman of the jury stood up to give the verdict, the credits began to roll. Rather than wait three days to find out, I set the chart.

I had no particular interest in Deirdre, so she is "any old person": 7th house. Had I strongly identified with her, perhaps having experienced something similar myself, she would be given the 1st house, as if the question were "Will we be sent down?" If I were strongly smitten with her, she would still be 7th, this time as the object of my affections.

Deirdre was already in prison, as she had been refused bail. Lord 7, Mars, shows this: it is in the turned 12th house (12 from 7th = radical 6th). It is in its own sign: lots of essential dignity, so Deirdre is innocent. But it is about to conjunct Saturn, which is in its fall and so is very nasty. It is also the natural ruler of imprisonment. Something horrible is going to happen to her: she will be convicted and sentenced to jail.

This is all happening in a cardinal sign, however, suggesting things that are quickly over. Once past Saturn, Mars hasn't far to travel before it enters Deirdre's 1st house. She is entering her own house. This, as so often in horary, can be taken literally: she will soon be coming home. Before Mars gets home it meets Mercury, which is retrograde: what has been said (Mercury) will change (retrograde). Someone's story will change, as a result of which Deirdre will be freed.

The South Node close to the cusp of the turned 11th (11 from 7th = radical 5th) shows where Deirdre will be hurt: through her friends. Although there is a moderately strong mutual reception between Mars and Jupiter, ruler of this house (each in the other's triplicity), they oppose each other by antiscion. It was the testimony of a friend that was crucial to her conviction. But the friends (Jupiter is in a double-bodied sign, so there is more than one) are honest (strong essential dignity), so the false testimony must have been given in error. Jupiter being a strongly dignified benefic, they will want to act for the best, and the mutual reception shows them helping.

Note here an example of that important point about mutual reception: it can work only to the extent that both planets are strong. Here both planets are strong, so the friends are capable of helping and Deirdre is capable of being helped.

To smooth the feathers of those horrified at the asking of so "trivial" a question - merriment being forbidden in some outposts of contemporary horary – I should add that Deirdre's imprisonment brought front-page headlines in the national press and questions in parliament. Not, perhaps, quite so trivial! The story unfolded as the chart shows.

Will Brazil Beat Argentina?

Leah Cuperman

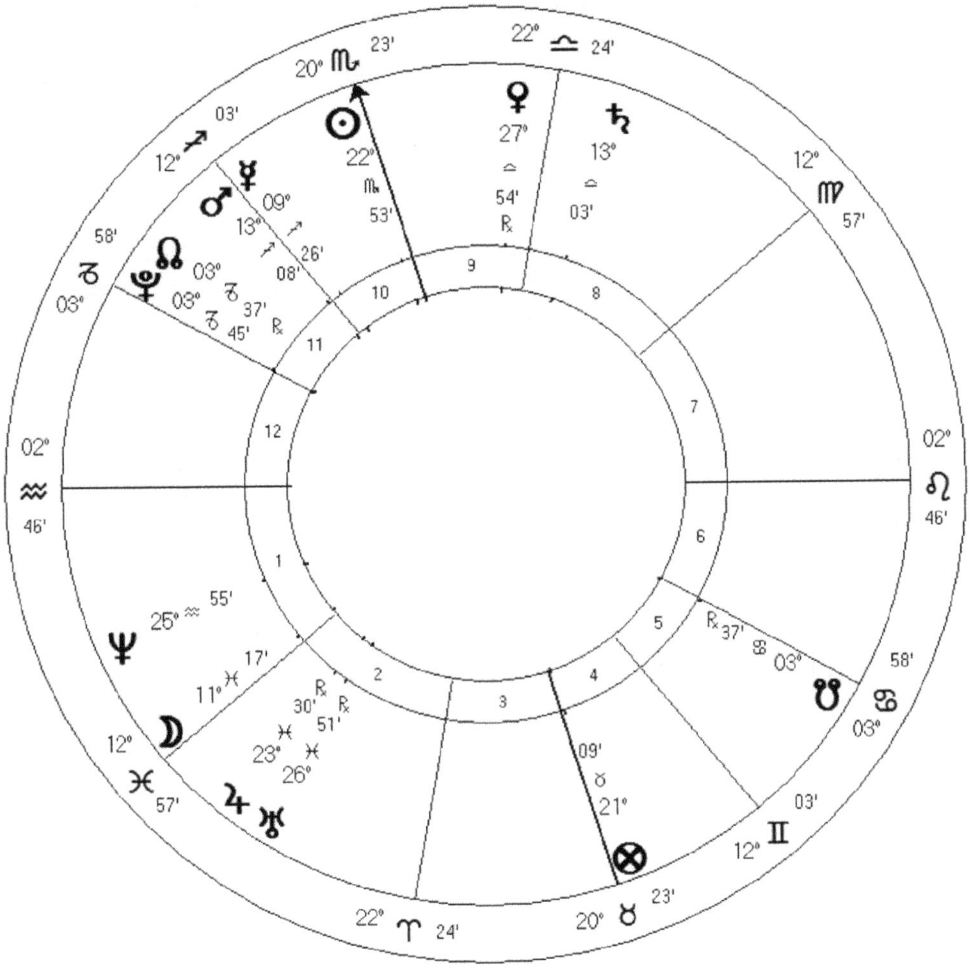

November 15, 2010, 11:15 A.M. | Herzliya, Israel | 2 Aquarius

Argentina was to play football against Brazil. The querent was a passionate supporter of Brazil and asked, "Will Brazil win in Wednesday's match?"

With such questions, it is vital that the querent have a genuine preference for one of the two teams. Otherwise, we have no criteria for deciding which team is shown by which house of the chart. Our querent was in effect asking "Will we win?", so the team she supports will be given the 1st house and its opponents the 7th (the enemies). In this chart, Brazil is signified by Lord 1, Saturn, at 13:03 Libra, and Argentina by the Sun at 22:53 Scorpio.

The first thing is to check if there is a planet strengthening or afflicting either of the two houses we are concerned with by its presence in that house. Here, there is no planet in either house. The Moon is not in the 1st because when a planet is fewer than 5 degrees from the cusp of the next house, it is considered to be in that next house. Being so close to the 2nd cusp, the Moon here is in the 2nd house and has no effect upon the 1st.

Second is to consider the strength of the significators. In these questions accidental dignity is much more important than essential dignity. Essential dignity shows the quality of the teams – which will play better – but it is accidental dignity that shows us who will win.

Saturn, significator of Brazil, is in its exaltation, showing the team will play at its very best. But being in the 8th, a weak house, is an accidental debility. The Sun, significator of Argentina, has no essential dignity: their performance will be poor. But it is very strong accidentally: its position conjunct the MC shows that Argentina are in charge.

And so it proved. Even though Brazil were the better team, Argentina beat them 1-0 with a goal in the last minute of the game.

Will Barrett Win?

Kathryn Silvestre

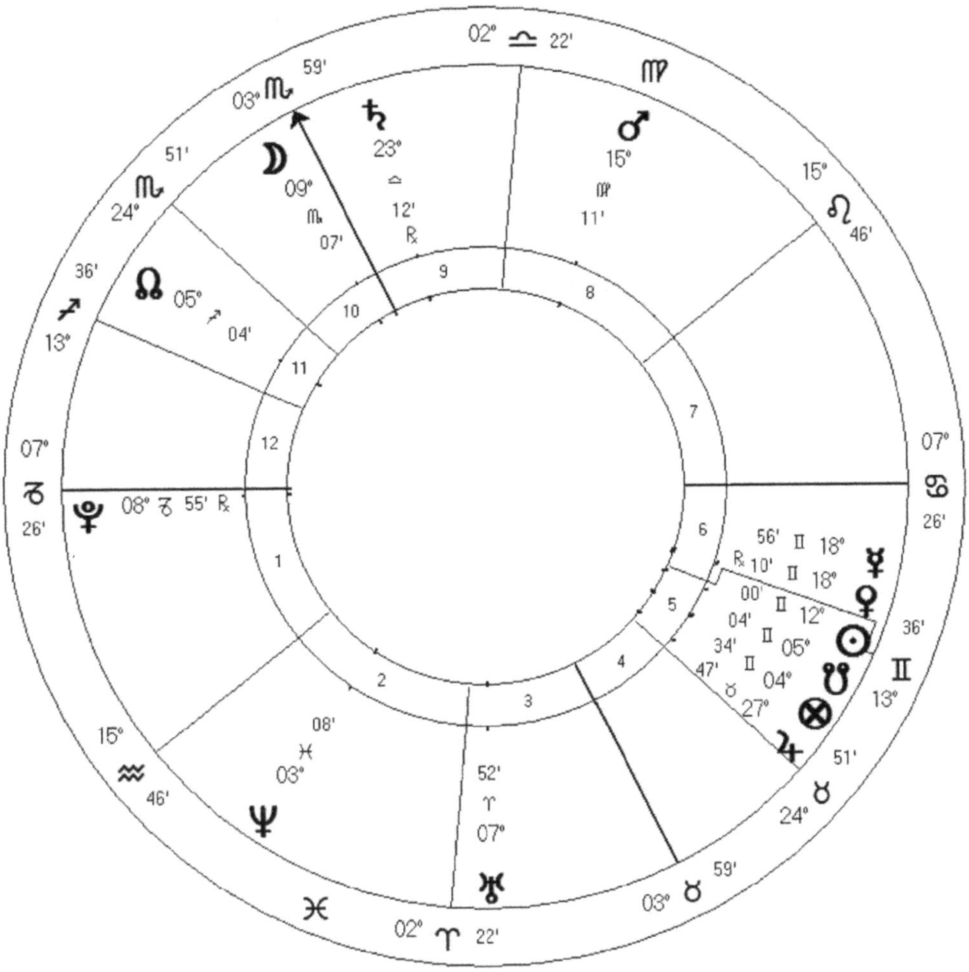

June 01, 2012, 10:15 P.M. | Wauwatosa, WI | 7 Capricorn

On June 5, 2012, Wisconsin held a special election to decide if Republican Governor Scott Walker would remain in power or be removed from office. Anti-Walker activists had collected over a million signatures for a recall election, in hopes of firing Walker and electing someone else. Walker's opponent in the recall was Tom Barrett, the same man who had lost to him in the general election two years earlier.

Election questions are a type of contest horary. We have a reigning governor here, Walker. As "king" he gets the 10th house and its lord, Mars.

What house signifies Barrett, his challenger? In order to determine this we must know the attitude of the querent. Is he or she partisan or indifferent? In this case, the querent self-identified as a Barrett supporter ("Will we win? "). Barrett then gets the 1st house and its lord, Saturn. If the querent didn't care either way, Barrett would be 4th house, Walker's opponent.

The Moon is the key to judgment in election horaries, as it signifies the electorate. If the Moon goes to aspect one of the two candidates, that candidate wins. At 9 Scorpio, the Moon's next aspect is a sextile with Mars at 15 Virgo: Walker will win. And he did, by a landslide.

Note, too, that the chart shows the electorate favoring Walker by reception (the Moon is in Scorpio, ruled by Mars). The reception is not needed for judgment, though. All we need is the aspect.

Will the Champion Retain His Belt?

Marcos Monteiro

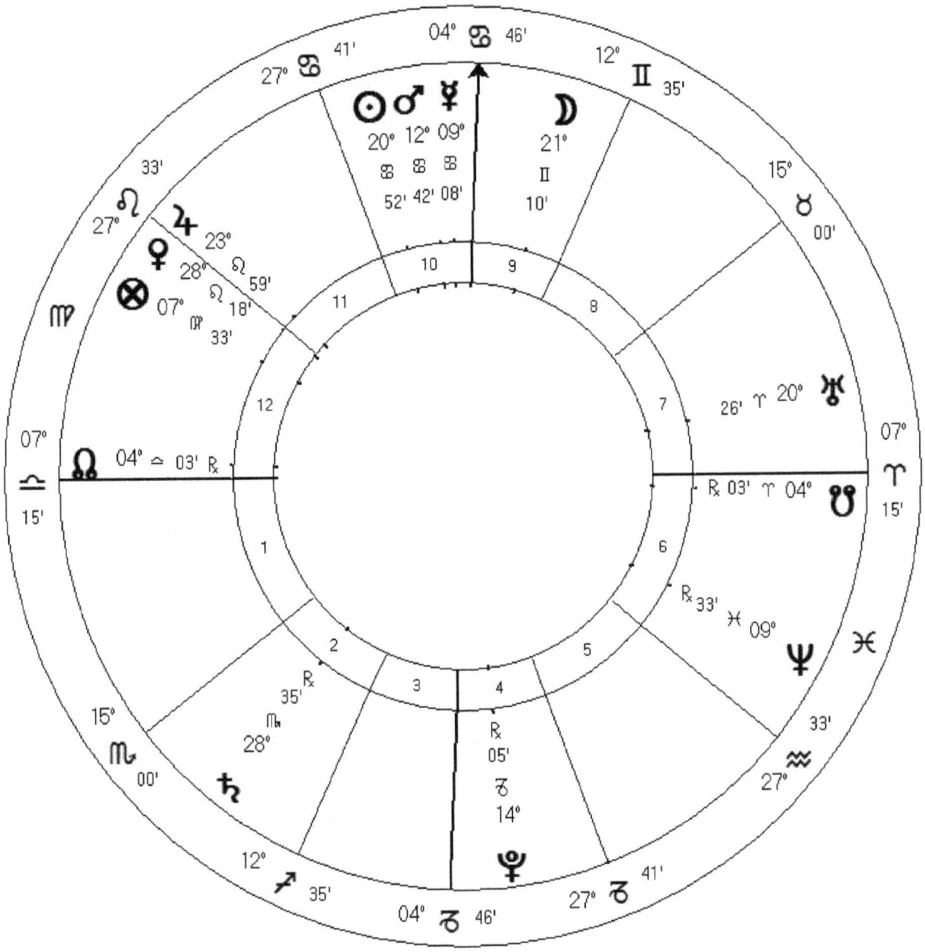

July 13, 2015, 11:11 A.M. | Barra Velha/SC, Brazil | 7 Libra

TJ Dillashaw shocked the MMA World when he took the UFC Bantamweight title from Renan Barão and ended his 33-fight, 9-year unbeaten streak.

They would fight again, and I wanted to know who would win this rematch.

Dillashaw is the champion, the current holder of the Bantamweight belt. There is an asymmetry here: it's not a championship in which people fight one another and someone wins it. He holds the belt until someone beats him, he retires, or is stripped from the title by the UFC; people fight for the chance of fighting him.

So, he's the king, and therefore signified by the ruler of the tenth house of kings, the Moon.

Barão is the challenger (the enemy of the king), signified by the fourth house, which opposes the tenth, and its ruler, Saturn.

Normally we give the Sun to the champion (as the natural ruler of kings) and the Moon to the challenger (as the natural ruler of the people), but not here: the Moon is already in use, and we cannot give two significators for one fighter and only one for the other; the Athletic Commission would not allow that.

What matters, here, is the accidental dignity of the planets – how they are acting now – not their essential dignity. We don't want to know who has the best genes, but who will come out on top in this particular event.

There is nothing happening to the houses' cusps themselves.

The Moon is in a neutral house, not afflicted by anything, but not in any way assisted, either. She suffers a little bit of harm by being in the ninth house, which is opposed to the third, the house of her joy.

Saturn is in a neutral house. It is in the Moon's fall, but that is irrelevant – neither of them has power over the other, and we would think that the challenger is not the greatest fan of the man who took his title from him. Saturn is also retrograde, but fighting is not a race; the direction the fighter goes doesn't have much to do with his ability to perform.

Saturn is applying to a very close square with Venus. Close aspects are considered influences in this kind of chart – but is it good or bad?

Venus is peregrine, neither in dignity or debility, so, it's hard to tell if it is working as a benefic or a malefic in general terms. It's just inside the twelfth cusp, but that could show restriction – Venus is not the ruler of the house, it just happens to be trapped in it.

But look at the receptions: Saturn is in Venus's detriment, Venus is in Saturn's detriment. This is not a good sign – Venus wants to bring Saturn down, so to speak.

So far the situation, as I see it, is marginally better for the champion; but it's not a very conclusive chart yet, and we're not done. We haven't yet analyzed a very important testimony.

There's something called antiscion in astrology, which is very important, but may seem somewhat odd to people that don't work with it.

Imagine a line passing through the 0 Cancer/ 0 Capricorn axis. It seems that any point in one side of this axis (say, in 10 Leo) has an alternative placement in the other side (20 Taurus). It's as if the planet was in both places. The bodily placement and the antiscion have some differences which we don't need to investigate now.

What we do need to investigate now is the antiscia of anything relevant to the question. Saturn gives us nothing, but the Moon's antiscion falls exactly on Mercury. The Moon's relationship with Mercury is exactly the opposite of Venus's relationship with Saturn – they love each other. So, although Mercury is not dignified, we could say this is a small help for the Moon.

But more importantly, the antiscion of the Moon falls just inside the tenth house, a little over four degrees from the cusp--close enough to make it angular, which is a very big accidental dignity. Now the scales seem to weigh more clearly in the champion's favor.

Judgment: The champion wins and retains his belt.

The champion convincingly beat his predecessor again, winning by technical knockout in the fourth round.

Has X Won the Election?

Fotini Christodoulou

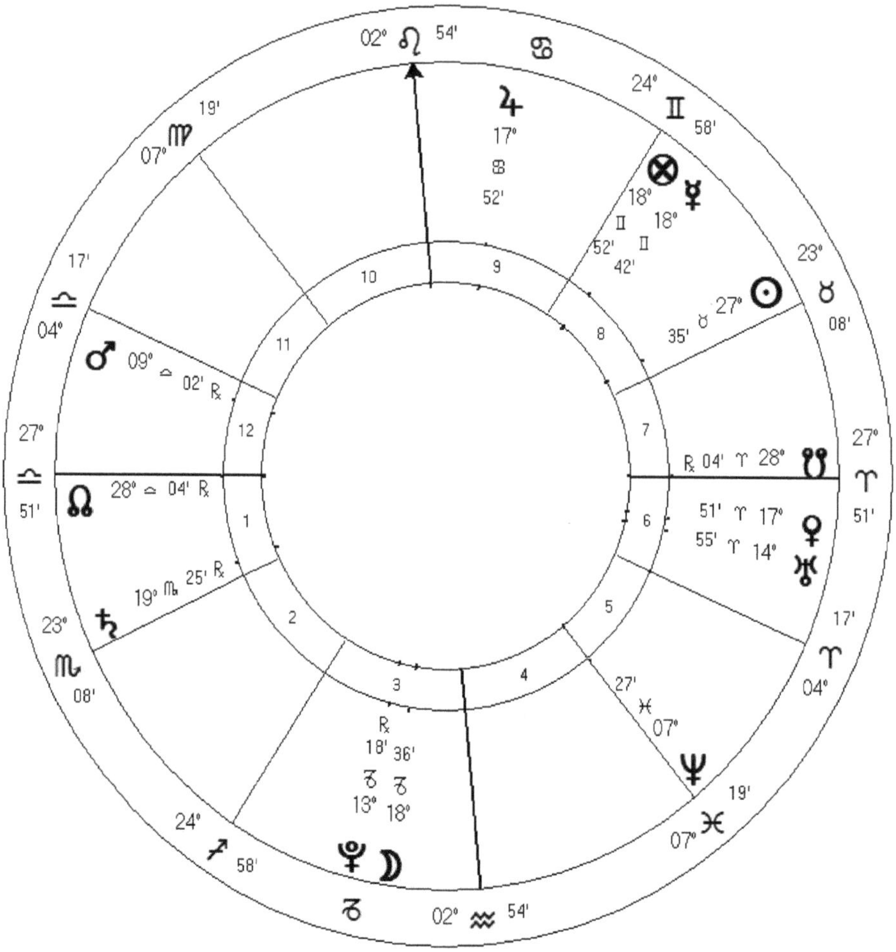

May 18, 2014, 6:04 P.M. | Thessaloniki, Greece | 27 Libra

The question was submitted right after the closure of the voting polls.

The querent wants to know whether the candidate he supports has won the election, so the candidate is signified by the Ascendant and Lord 1. The Moon will signify the voters, the people.

It is important to point out that in this particular case we are concerned with the Moon's last aspect and not the future one; that because, the electoral procedure was completed and despite the fact that the votes are not yet counted, the result is already there.

We can see that the Ascendant is conjunct the North Node and this is a very good first indication. Lord 1 is Venus and the "enemy" is Mars. So what we need is to check the Moon's last aspect that will show which one has won.

We can see that the Moon is separating from Jupiter which is neither of the relevant significators. If we look carefully though, we can see that Venus is immediately applying to perfect an aspect to Jupiter. This Jupiter is a slow planet in relevance to both the Moon and Venus: this is what we call a collection of light; Jupiter collects their light and is bringing them together in a sense. So, the querent's favorite has won the election. And so it proved.

Will Romney Win the US Presidency?

Kathryn Silvestre

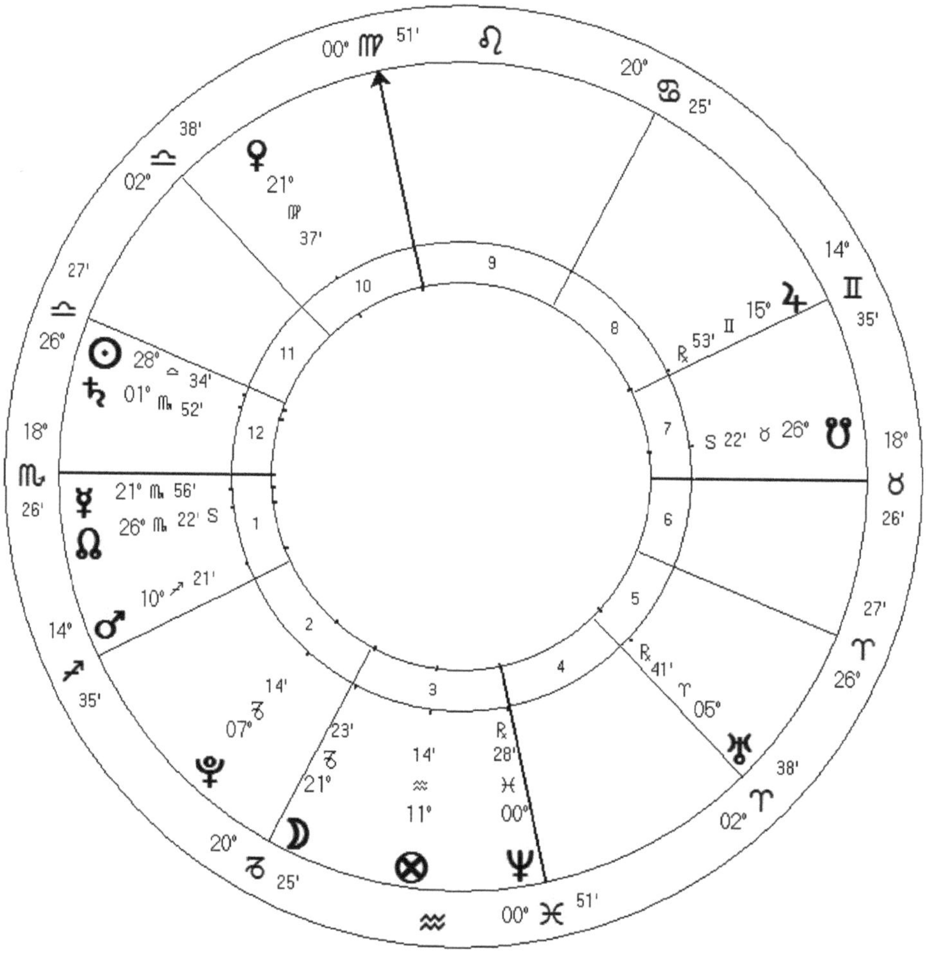

October 21, 2012, 9:02 A.M. | Wauwatosa, WI | 18 Scorpio

Election questions are a subset of contest horaries, with a few special considerations depending upon who is asking the question. House assignment must be teased out carefully in order to reach correct judgment.

House assignment is easily handled if the election is in one's own country and the querent has a strong allegiance to one candidate. In such a case, the querent's candidate gets the first house, in the same way that the querent's team gets the first house in a sports horary. This is because the querent identifies so strongly with the team or candidate that it's as if they are one and the same ("we"). If the opponent is currently in power he gets the tenth house; if not, he gets the seventh. Judgment proceeds from there.

But what happens when the querent's feelings are mixed? Or when she dislikes both candidates, but has voted consistently with one party over the other? Such was the situation when I asked this question prior to the US Presidential Election in 2012. It was shared originally with a community of colleagues online and inspired some debate.

Although I had voted for Obama in 2008, I was strongly disappointed in him. On the other hand, I certainly did not support Mitt Romney, his opponent. So was Obama my candidate, or wasn't he?

We must think of this logically: in the absence of strong feelings of support for Obama, he cannot be "my candidate," 1st house. If he cannot be the 1st house, then as the current officeholder he must be the 10th. Romney must then be the 4th house as his opponent.

Virgo is on the cusp of the 10th house, therefore Obama is signified by Mercury, ruler of Virgo. Pisces is the sign on the cusp of the 4th house, opposite. Romney then is signified by Jupiter, ruler of Pisces.

In election horaries the Moon, natural ruler of the people, signifies the electorate. If the Moon applies to aspect one of the significators, that candidate wins. In this chart the Moon applies immediately to trine Venus, after which it immediately sextiles Mercury, signifying Obama.

Now, what is Venus? We don't know, and it doesn't matter. What does matter is whether Venus has any power to prohibit the aspect with Mercury that follows. The Moon to Mercury means a win for Obama, unless the trine with Venus prohibits (stops the Moon from reaching Mercury).

Venus is in Virgo and therefore disposes to Mercury, ruler of that sign. This means that Mercury has power over Venus; he rules her. Because Venus is ruled by Mercury, she cannot prohibit the Moon's sextile with Mercury: Obama will win. This was my prediction, and it proved correct.

It seems relevant that Mercury is in a fixed sign here, well away from the end of the sign. But this is not necessary for judgment. The Moon going to Mercury, after trine with a non-prohibiting Venus, is all we need.

Will Brazil Win the 2014 World Cup?

Marcos Monteiro

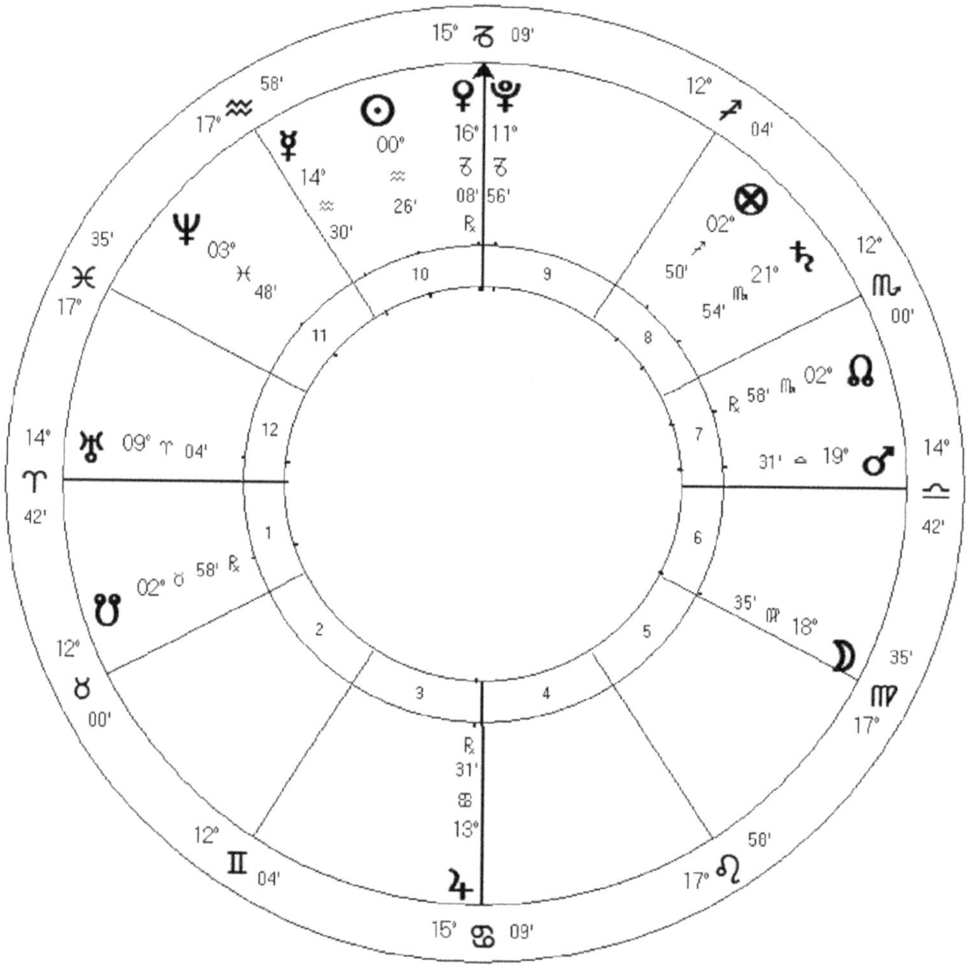

January 20, 2014, 12:21 P.M. | Barra Velha/SC, Brazil | 14 Aries

Being the 2014 FIFA World Football Cup hosts, and also being the only team to have won it five times, Brazil was one of the obvious favorites, if not the favorite, to win the Cup again.

The thing is, our team was not one to make us sure of anything. They were, of course, good, but they were not great, and it would take more than just that – even with the home advantage – to beat the very best of the world.

So, I wanted to know if we would make it, if we would win the Cup at home.

The querent – me – is signified by Mars, ruler of the sign on the first house cusp (the house that signifies the querent, the person that asks the question).

It also means the Brazilian team.

It does so because the querent is not only Brazilian, but identifies himself with the team. I wouldn't do it with the Water Polo team, though – I would certainly say "they're good, they have won" or "they're bad, they have lost" when referring to them. But I say, as most Brazilians do, "we won" or "we lost" when our team plays.

The team, then, is an "extended us", and is therefore signified by Mars. It is not, however, co-signified by the Moon. The Moon means the querent, sure, but it's especially related to the querent's feelings and, consequently, is personal. I don't share my feelings on everything (probably not even on the Cup) with the Brazilian team.

Mars is in Libra, its detriment, which is not good; but it's not relevant here. The question is not about which team is the best in general. Moreover, I knew the team was not spectacular; that's why I asked the question.

I'd like to see an aspect between us (Mars) and the ruler of the tenth, Saturn, "the victory". I don't just want to see Mars strong accidentally (which could mean we would play good football); there are a lot of good teams out there, but only one will get their hands on the trophy.

There is a very nice reception between Mars and Saturn. Mars in Libra exalts Saturn, which we already know – we would like very much to be the ones who lift up the Cup – and Saturn is in the sign of Mars. This could mean Saturn loves Mars, but that makes no sense in this context. Victory (or, at least, Victory's heart) is as blind as Justice. Here, it describes the situation: the Cup is taking place here, at our home.

This reception means nothing, then: we must have an aspect. And there is none. Saturn and Mars are in adjacent signs: an aspect is impossible.

We don't need anything else for our judgment, but there is more. There is another planet (Venus) close to the tenth cusp (another team is getting there), a small testimony against us, and another planet (the Moon) is about to aspect Saturn (another team is getting their hands on the trophy), a big testimony against us.

Brazil will not win the World Cup.

Although it seemed increasingly unlikely as the Cup progressed and we advanced, Brazil suffered an unprecedented defeat against Germany (1 to 7) in the semifinals. Germany advanced to beat Argentina and become the 2014 World Cup winner.

Will the Brewers Make the Playoffs?

Kathryn Silvestre

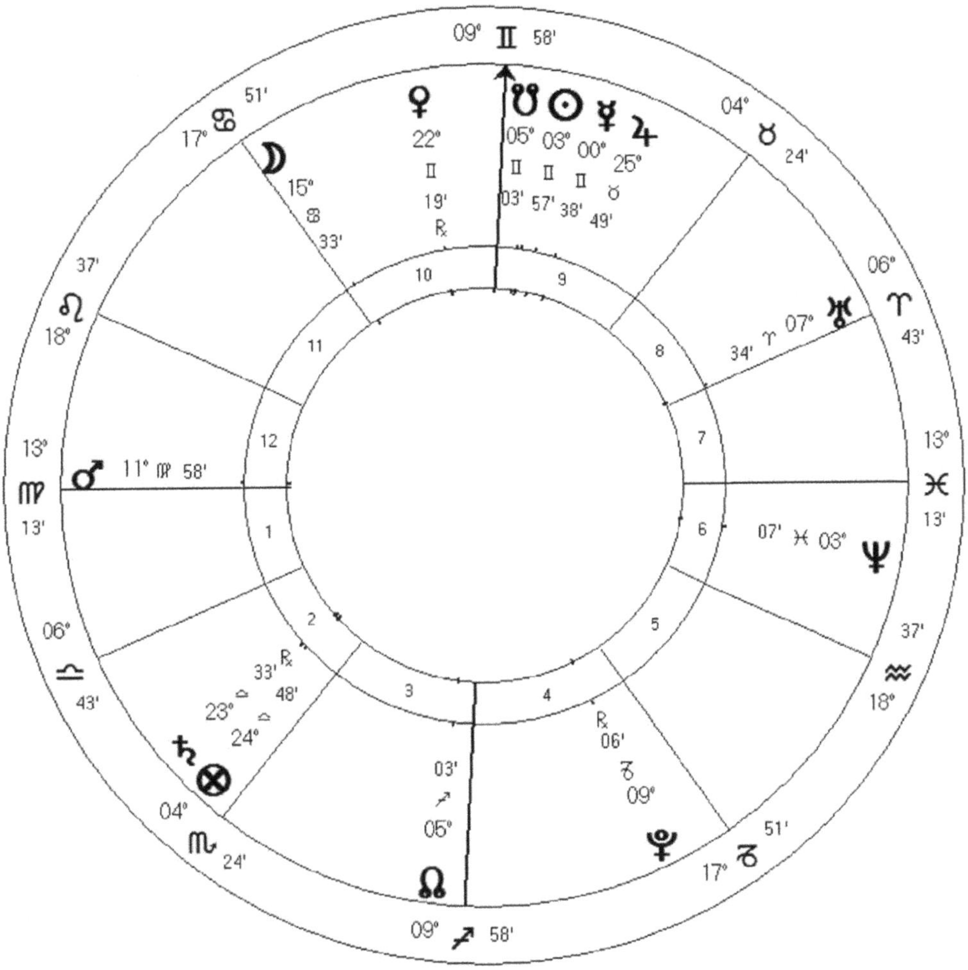

May 24, 2012, 1:14 P.M. | Milwaukee, WI | 13 Virgo

The querent was an avid Brewers baseball fan, asking how the team would fare for the remainder of the season. The club was playing much worse than hoped for after a strong season the previous year.

Because the querent identifies the Brewers as his team they are Lord 1, Mercury, ruler of Virgo on the Ascendant. Mercury is at the very beginning of Gemini, which it rules (along with Virgo). Mercury, therefore, is essentially very strong. We might think this is positive testimony in itself; however, Mercury's present condition shows the team now. We know the team is not doing very well just now. What we need to know is where Mercury will go from here. Is there anything ahead to suggest things getting substantially better for Mercury in the current sign? We limit our view to Mercury while it is in Gemini, as this signifies the current season.

Mercury is combust here: within seven and a half degrees of the Sun and, in this case, applying to conjunction with the Sun. Normally combustion is destructive – one of the worst things that can happen to a planet. But when a planet is combust while in its own sign, the combustion acts instead like a mutual reception. We could argue this is a positive testimony, as if something is in the team's corner lending assistance. We don't need to define what this might be: it could be a number of things.

However, the next thing ahead for Mercury is the South Node. This is a definite negative testimony. The South Node diminishes: not what we're looking for in a team aspiring to the playoffs. There is nothing else ahead while Mercury is in Gemini to suggest things will improve for the team. With nothing shouting Yes, and one clear testimony for No, the more reasonable answer is No, the Brewers won't make the playoffs. And they did not.

When Will I Win the Money from This Trial?

Marcos Monteiro

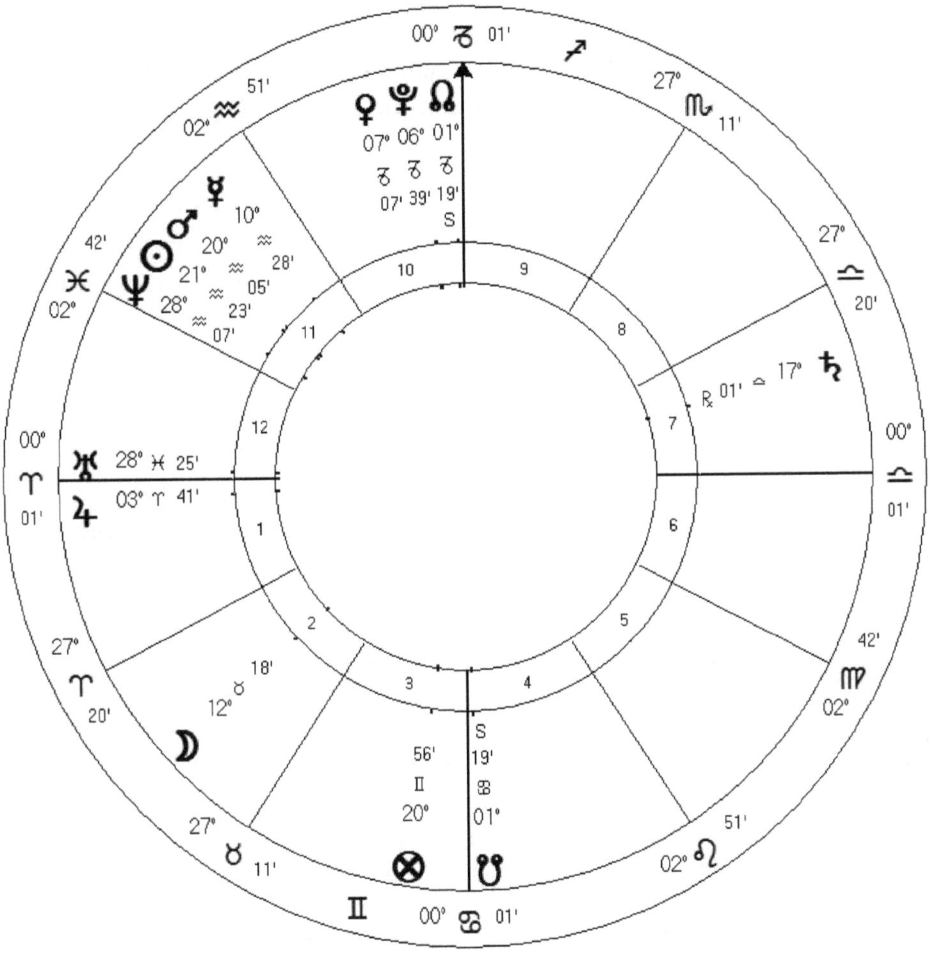

February 10, 2011, 9:54 A.M. | Barra Velha/SC, Brazil | 0 Aries

This is an interesting chart for a variety of reasons.

The querent was suing a telecom company, in what he and his lawyer believed was an easy trial. Neither of them had any doubt that they would win: however, after two years, the querent started to wonder when it would happen.

The querent is Mars, ruler of Aries; the telecom company is Venus, ruler of Libra (the 7th house is the house of open enemies). The judge in the case is Saturn, ruler of the tenth house.

The verdict in a civil trial is Lord 4: here, the Moon. The Moon will make a square to Mars in about eight degrees, so all we have to do is to choose the unit to tell the client when he'll win. Or, it would be so, if things were that simple.

Every genuine horary chart reflects the real situation as seen from the client's perspective. That's important: it's the client's perspective, but it's life as it is, not as he/she would like it to be.

If a querent asks "when", we do not need to ask "if", because it's given in the question. But people make assumptions that sometimes are not true, and if the chart tells us that the "if" is not that all certain, we must hear it.

This chart clearly gives us some warnings. First, Mars, the querent, is combust in Aquarius. It's no big deal to be in the sign of the judge; we know the querent (and his opponents) are in the judge's power. But it is a big deal to be combust by a detrimented Sun, a bad Sun blinding Mars. It's a very clear sign that the querent is not seeing the situation. More than that, Mars is very weak, as combustion is one of the worse afflictions possible in the sky.

If the rest of the chart supported the querent's version, maybe we could disregard that; but I don't think that's the case.

First, Saturn is in Libra. It's not important that he is a good judge: we are not concerned with his overall judging abilities, but whether he'll grant our querent his wishes. In Libra, the judge is not willing to do so: he is in the sign of Venus, our enemies, and in the detriment of Mars. He loves the company and hates our querent.

The ruler of the company, Venus, is in Capricorn. It's very interesting that Venus is the only planet liking Mars – it could mean they would settle for an agreement. But it's also in the sign of Saturn, ensuring the enemies and the judge have mutual reception (common interests). On top of that, Venus is heading to a mutually applying square with Saturn. Mercury seems to prohibit that aspect, getting to Saturn first; however (we discuss that below), while this may spoil the aspect between them, it does not change their mutual inclinations.

The Moon, too, is in the detriment of Mars. The verdict does not like or hate anyone, but it can harm people. Here, harming Mars is not a good testimony. Aspects are opportunities to act; an aspect between a combust planet and an another planet which hates it is a bad opportunity at best.

But it gets worse. The antiscion of Mercury is at 19:32 Scorpio. The Moon hits Mercury before reaching Mars. This opposition by antiscion (contrantiscion, as it is called in ancient texts), prohibits the Moon-Mars aspect and clears the way for the Venus-Saturn aspect (it prohibits the prohibition, as it were).

The chart is clearly telling us the querent will not win at all. The querent did not believe the judgment, and asked for a timing anyway. From the nature of the situation, I judged that the almost eight degrees the Moon takes to perfect the aspect with Mars meant eight months, still thinking it was unlikely that he would win.

Around one year later, in an audience with a mediator, the telecom company offered an agreement, which the querent refused to accept because the amount offered was too low.

The querent later lost the trial.

Will the Badgers Win the Rose Bowl?

Kathryn Silvestre

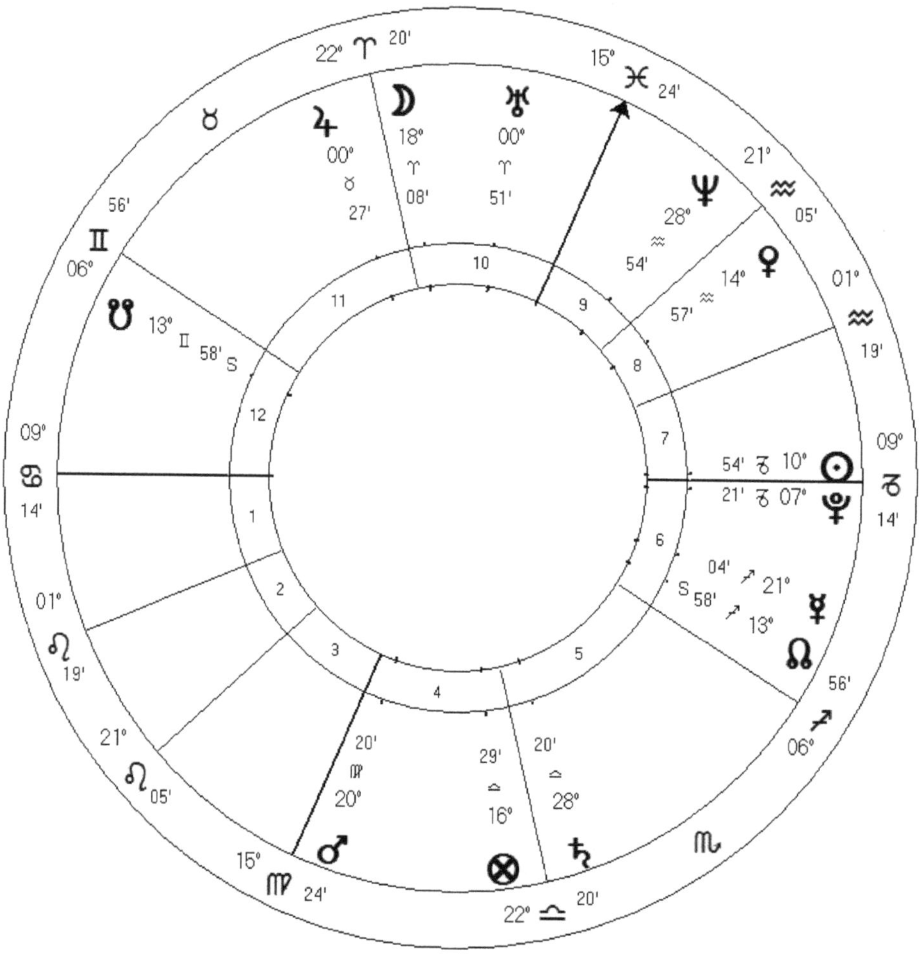

January 01, 2012, 4:14 P.M. | Milwaukee, WI | 19 Cancer

I'm a sports fan, college sports especially. My alma mater is the University of Wisconsin Madison. Madison teams are known as the Badgers. For three years in a row, beginning in 2011, the football Badgers earned a trip to the Rose Bowl. I asked this question the day before the big game in January 2012.

The Badgers are my team, so "we" are Lord 1. Cancer rises in this chart, making the Moon significator of the Badgers. Oregon, the opponent, is signified by Saturn, ruler of Capricorn on the seventh cusp.

This is a quick chart to judge. Saturn, Oregon, is exalted. Exaltation in sports horaries means the team is as strong as it can be. Exaltation is even stronger than sign rulership, which is not the case in other contexts.

The Moon has no essential dignity where it is in Aries, so it is no match for Saturn. From this chart I predicted that Oregon would win the Rose Bowl, and so they did.

That's pretty much the story! It's worth mentioning a few minor points, though. First, accidental dignity in sports horaries is more important than essential dignity. Here, though, both planets are in neutral houses: the fifth and the eleventh. This offers us nothing to weigh against our main testimony in favor of Oregon.

The antiscion of the South Node falls in the first house, North Node in the seventh. Together, this counts as one minor testimony against the Badgers and for Oregon.

What about the Sun and Pluto sitting just above and just below the Descendant, respectively? Both should be afflictions – the Sun because it is peregrine, and Pluto because it is Pluto, nasty in most contexts. Neither seems to have had any negative effect on Oregon, however, when weighed against Saturn's exaltation.

Money & Jobs

Will I Get a Good Yearly Review of My Work?

Leah Cuperman

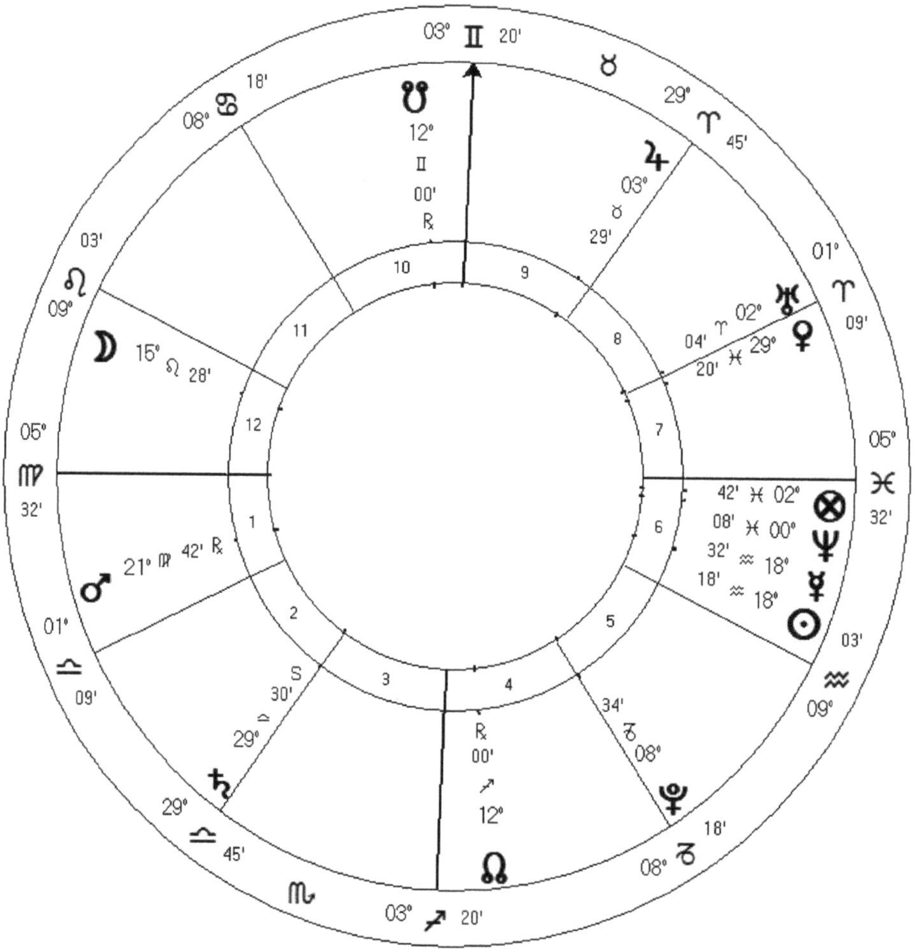

February 07, 2012, 6:37 P.M. | Herzliya, Israel | 5 Virgo

Some charts are beautiful in their simplicity, and this is a fine example.

Before the annual meeting with her boss, the querent asked, “Will I get a good yearly review of my work?”

The querent is signified by Lord 1, Mercury, at 18:32 Aquarius and the Moon at 15:28 Leo.

Mercury is only 14' away from the Sun. The area that comprises 17½' of the Sun is known as "cazimi" and is of great power. It is traditionally likened to someone being raised to sit next to the king.

This gives the full answer to the question. We don't even need to look at Lord 10, which would signify her boss, because the idea of being raised up by the king gives a perfect symbolic picture of her finding favor with the person at the top. She will have an excellent yearly review.

And so it proved. A few weeks later she wrote to confirm that the review could not have been any better.

Will My Tenant Send Full Payment?

Kathryn Silvestre

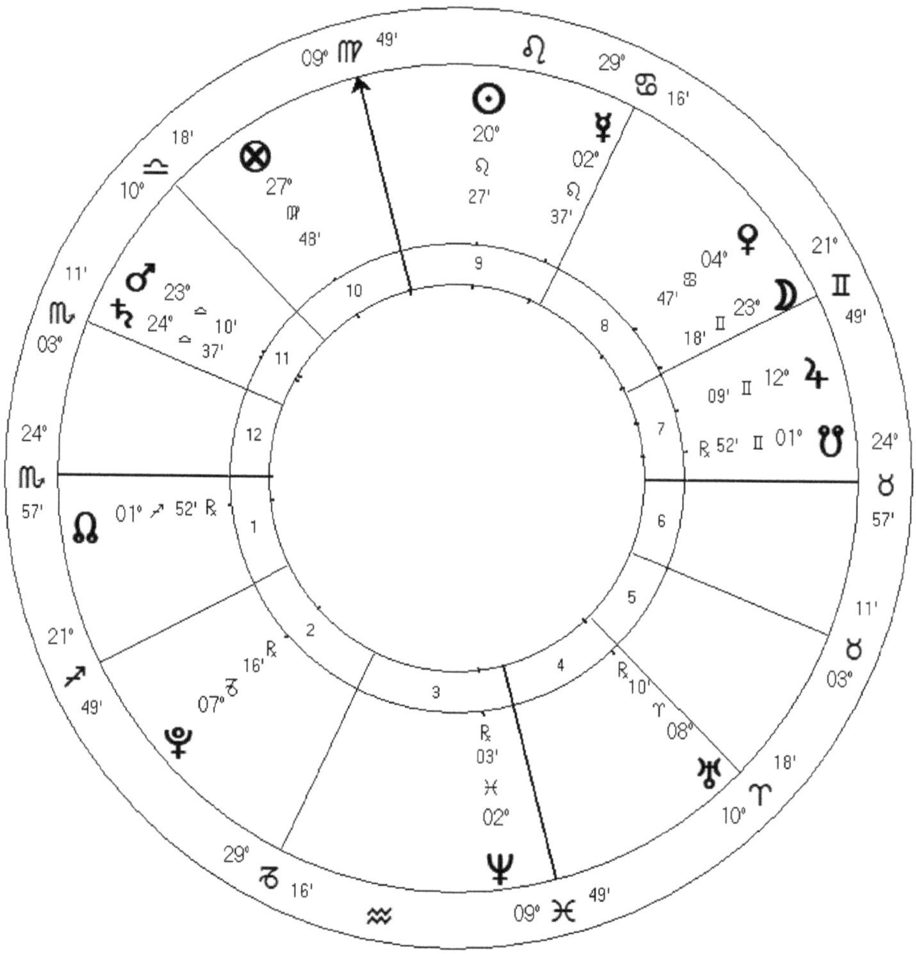

August 12, 2012, 2:11 P.M. | Wauwatosa, WI | 24 Scorpio

The querent had a tenant who was several months behind on rent and was being evasive when she raised the matter. The querent came for consultation to help her decide whether to proceed with eviction. She wanted to know if the tenant would pay the arrears due within the time limit she had set, which was one week.

The querent is Mars, ruler of Scorpio, the sign on the Ascendant. Her cosignificator is the Moon. The tenant is Lord 7, Venus, ruler of Taurus on the Descendant. Tenant's money – the key issue – is Lord 8, Mercury, ruler of Gemini on cusp eight. The question has two parts: 1) Does the tenant have enough money, and 2) Will she send it on time?

In order to judge the question we need to see at what shape the tenant's money is in. Mercury has no essential dignity where it is at present (2 Leo). This tells us very clearly that she doesn't have enough money to pay the full amount.

Will the tenant send the querent whatever amount she does have, within a week's time? To judge this we look to see if there is an applying aspect between Mercury, the tenant's money, and the querent herself, Mars, or her bank account, Lord 2. Lord 2 is Jupiter, ruler of Sagittarius on cusp two.

There is no aspect between Mercury and Mars. There is, however, an applying aspect between Mercury and Jupiter, the querent's bank account. Mercury will perfect a sextile with Jupiter when it reaches 13 Leo and Jupiter reaches 13 Gemini: 11 degrees. That this number is greater than one, and greater than seven, suggested to me that the money would not be sent within one week's time (seven days). I told the querent that her tenant had some money, but not the full amount, and that she would not send it within a week's time. The prediction was correct.

Will I Get the Job at UW?

Molly Morrissey

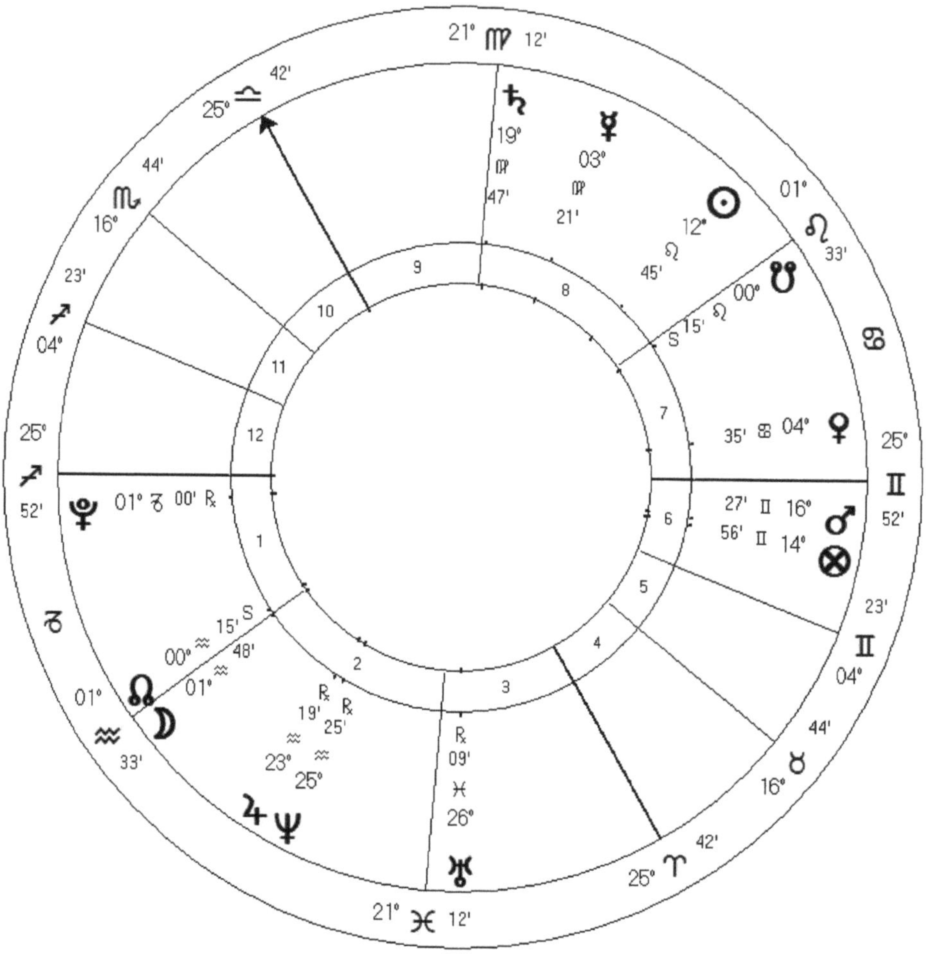

August 04, 2009, 5:49 P.M. | Redmond, WA | 25 Sagittarius

I had applied for a job as graduate student counselor and had gotten through the initial interviews. It was between me and another person. I also knew that there was no one who covertly already had the position, which is often the case in academia and government.

I was an exact fit for the description of the job, having not only received my undergraduate degree from that very department, but I also had the guidance counselor skills that the position wanted in addition to the industry and departmental knowledge. Not only that, but the professor who'd at one time held the position was still a close friend and had endorsed me within the department for the job. From all indicators, I was a shoe-in.

I am the querent and am signified by Lord 1, Jupiter, and the Moon. The job is Lord 10, Venus. My competition for the job is Lord 7, Mercury. I am looking to see who gets to Lord 10 first. Lord 7 makes a sextile to Lord 10, perfecting in about 5 degrees. Lord 10 is sitting in the 7th house, also a negative testimony for me. The job was in the other person's pocket.

And so it proved. The other person got the job.

But why? I thought I was a shoe-in for a variety of reasons. Apparently they had decided late in the game that knowledge of university administrative policy was the most important piece. This was the one bit of experience I did not have. Lord 7, Mercury, is strong in its own sign of Virgo: an apt picture of a university bureaucrat. Also, antiscion Venus sits right on the 7th house cusp, testimony that there was indeed a covert connection between the competitor and the position. It turned out that because she was already a university employee, there was a pre-existing bias. My significators are either peregrine or are retrograde with only minor dignity, which was confusing to me at the time since I thought I was qualified. The chart knew better – that in reality I was not qualified at all. So even though they knew and liked me (Lord 10, Venus, loves the Moon and exalts Jupiter) this had nothing to do with me getting the position. Not only that, but Venus does not behold my two significators. They don't even see me at all in relation to the job.

Will I Profit from This Bet?

Marcos Monteiro

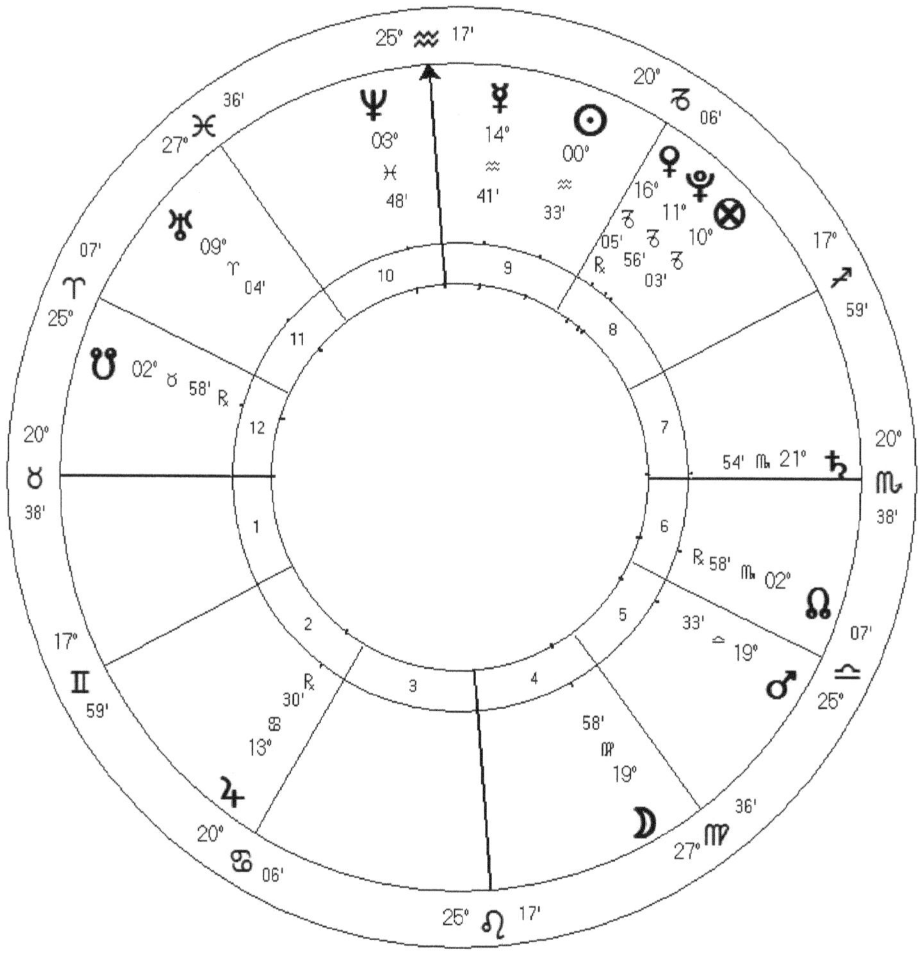

January 20, 2014, 3:05 P.M. | Barra Velha/SC, Brazil | 20 Taurus

I had cast a horary on the World Cup and saw that Brazil (the favorites) would not win. I was discussing with a friend, and she said she would bet on "any South American team" to win. I had some money on the betting site; it seemed a reasonable bet at that time (Argentina was the second best regarded team, and there were other strong ones from the continent). However, Europe was, as always, a probable origin of the champions.

So, I wanted to know if I would win this bet.

I'm Venus, Lord 1, and the Moon. My money is Mercury, Lord 2. The money from betting is Jupiter, Lord 8, the money from the betting site – Lord 7, my enemies in that context.

To answer "yes", I must see a connection between Lord 8 and either Lord 1, Lord 2, or the Moon.

The Moon won't aspect or conjunct any planet before it changes sign. It's void of course. We can eliminate that possibility.

Mercury is in a sign that does not behold Jupiter: they cannot aspect one another. No planet collects or translates light between then, either.

Jupiter and Venus seem to be heading for an opposition. Both are retrograde but Venus is faster; it will reach Jupiter eventually, so we have to decide if this opposition by retrograde planets is enough to give a "yes".

No, we don't: Venus stops before reaching Jupiter.

No aspect: it's a "no".

A European team, Germany, won the Cup. The bet would have given me nothing; I would have lost.

Should I Make This Trip or Open a Co-Working Spot?

Marcos Monteiro

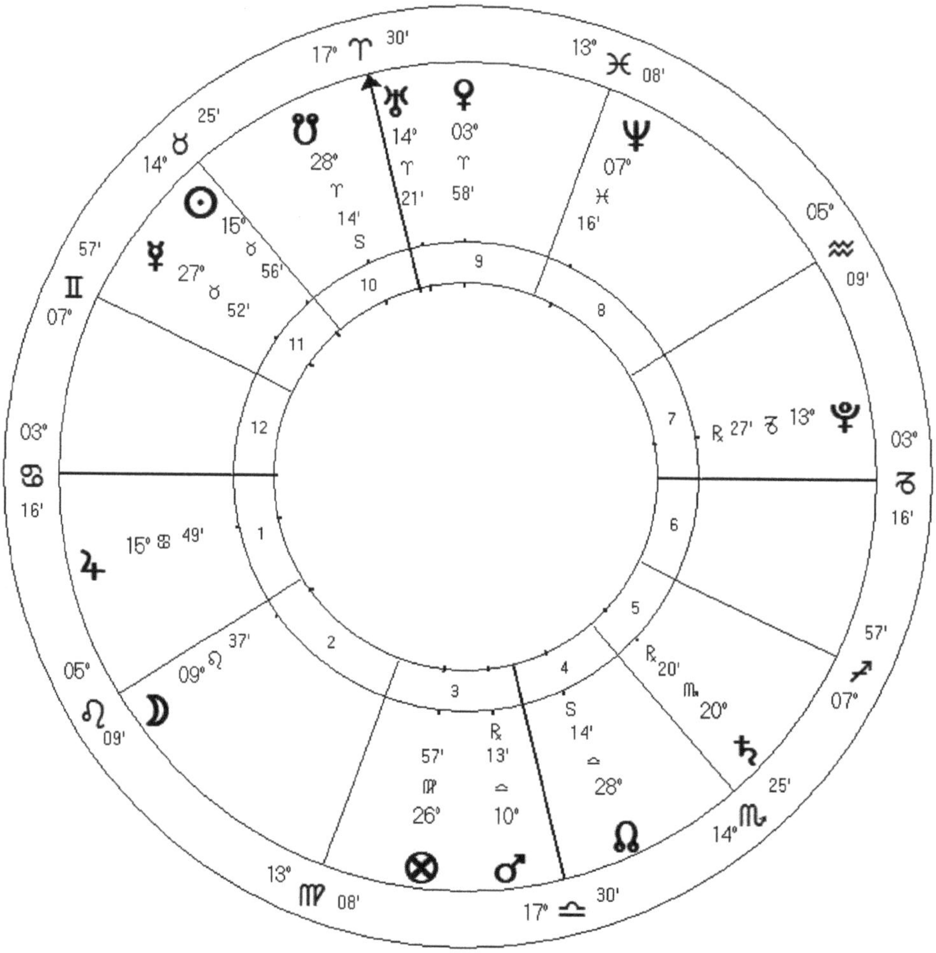

May 06, 2014, 10:22 A.M. | Barra Velha/SC, Brazil | 3 Cancer

The querent was closing a business and wanted to take a trip, to forget about work for a while.

However, she felt some pressure from family and friends, who though she should be doing some productive work, and was afraid that she could be letting a business opportunity slip from her hands.

She had this idea of renting a place and turn it into a co-working spot (a place where people could come and work on their laptops, or maybe on the place's own computers, for a fee – a "social" alternative for home offices). She had been researching this for a while and thought her city needed a place like that. If the business was a bad idea, however, she would rather spend some of the money that remained from the last business on a trip abroad and think about what she would do later.

The querent is Lord 1, the Moon.

The business is Lord 10; the profit from it is Lord 11. The trip would be Lord 9, but we really don't need this planet; the querent wanted to take the trip anyway.

We have to evaluate the business idea to see if it's a good one. Lord 10, Mars, is in its detriment in Libra. It's at 10 degrees, moving retrograde, and will soon station direct: as far as we are concerned, it will stay in Libra forever: not a good sign.

Lord 11, Venus, the potential profit from the business, is also in its detriment, in the early degrees of Aries: not a good sign.

The Moon aspects Mars and then heads towards the Sun, Lord 2, the querent's own money, translating the light between them. Mars is in Libra, the fall of the Sun: the Moon, the querent, connects her money and the business... and the business brings her money down. This is a big "no" – a clear sign that she should not start this business, traveling or not.

OK: The business is not a good idea. This pretty much is the answer: she was going to travel anyway.

But let's see how the trip would go. Lord 9 is Jupiter, very dignified in Cancer. Jupiter is exalted – the trip probably won't be as good as she was dreaming it would be, but that's not the journey's fault; reality usually is not as rosy as our best dreams.

But more than that, Jupiter is in the Moon's sign. It loves the Moon and wants to help her: the trip is a good thing for her.

The querent went abroad and told me afterwards that she had a very nice time. She had no regrets about not opening what didn't seem such good an idea anymore.

Should I Start This Business?

Leah Cuperman

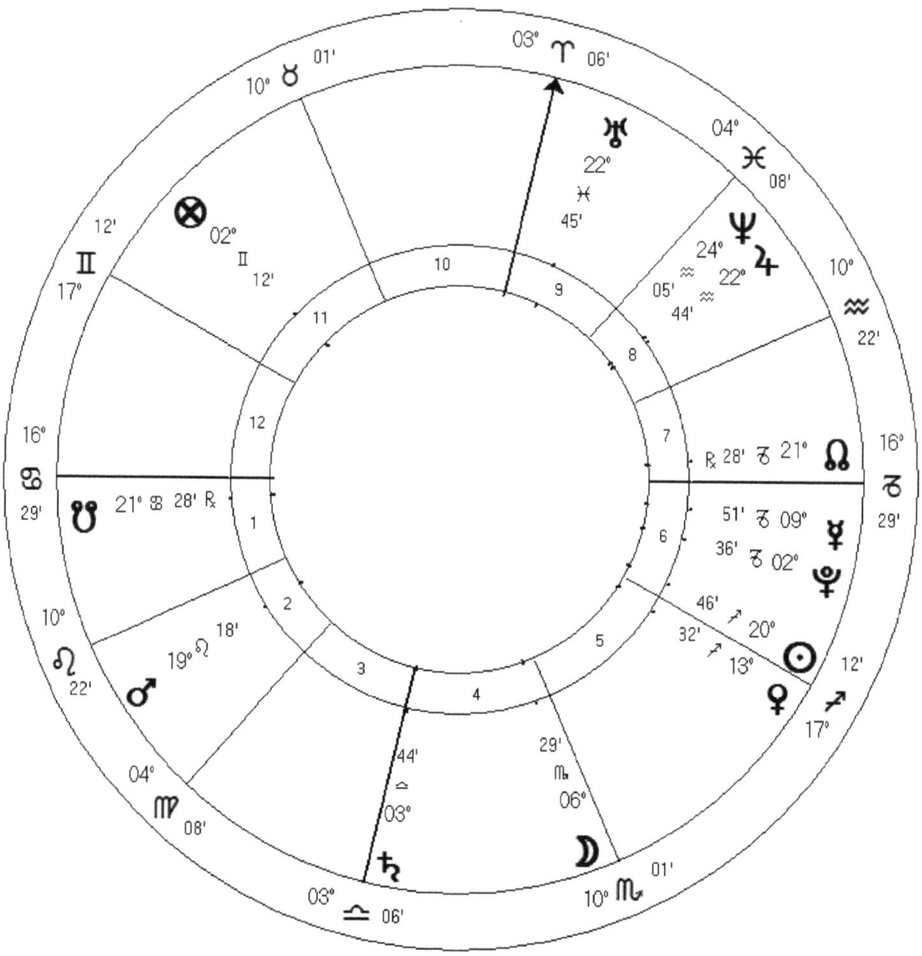

December 12, 2009, 6:26 P.M. | Herzliya, Israel | 16 Cancer

The person asking this question was planning to start a business.

His question was: Should I start this business? Will the profit be good?

The potential business that the querent has in mind is signified by the 10th house, which is ruled by Mars at 19:18 Leo.

Just as the radical 2nd house signifies the money of the querent, the 2nd from the 10th (or radical 11th house) shows the business's money, meaning the profit from the business.

In this case, the profit is signified by Venus at 13:32 Sagittarius. It has dignity by term, which is OK, but not particularly good. But at less than 8½ degrees from the Sun it is combust, which is very bad news for the querent.

What is going on with the potential clients? They are signified by Lord 7, Saturn at 3:44 Libra, and so is their money (radical 8th house or turned 2nd from the 7th). Saturn is exalted, which shows the clients have enough money to buy the products; but the fact that Saturn is not only in the detriment of Mars, but exactly opposing its cusp, highlights that they are not interested in the products and this, therefore, harms the business. Had Mars and Saturn been applying to an aspect, the lack of good reception would have given us the same answer.

Mars at 19:18 Leo has no essential dignity and is conjunct the 11th cusp by antiscion, afflicting that house. This shows that the poor quality of the business will afflict the profits.

The chart has enough testimonies to show that starting this business will not be worth it, as the profit will be very low.

The querent ignored the astrological advice and opened the business, but the prediction proved correct. He found it hard to get good customers; and to avoid losing money he was reduced to selling his stock at cost price.

When Will We Get Paid from X?

Fotini Christodoulou

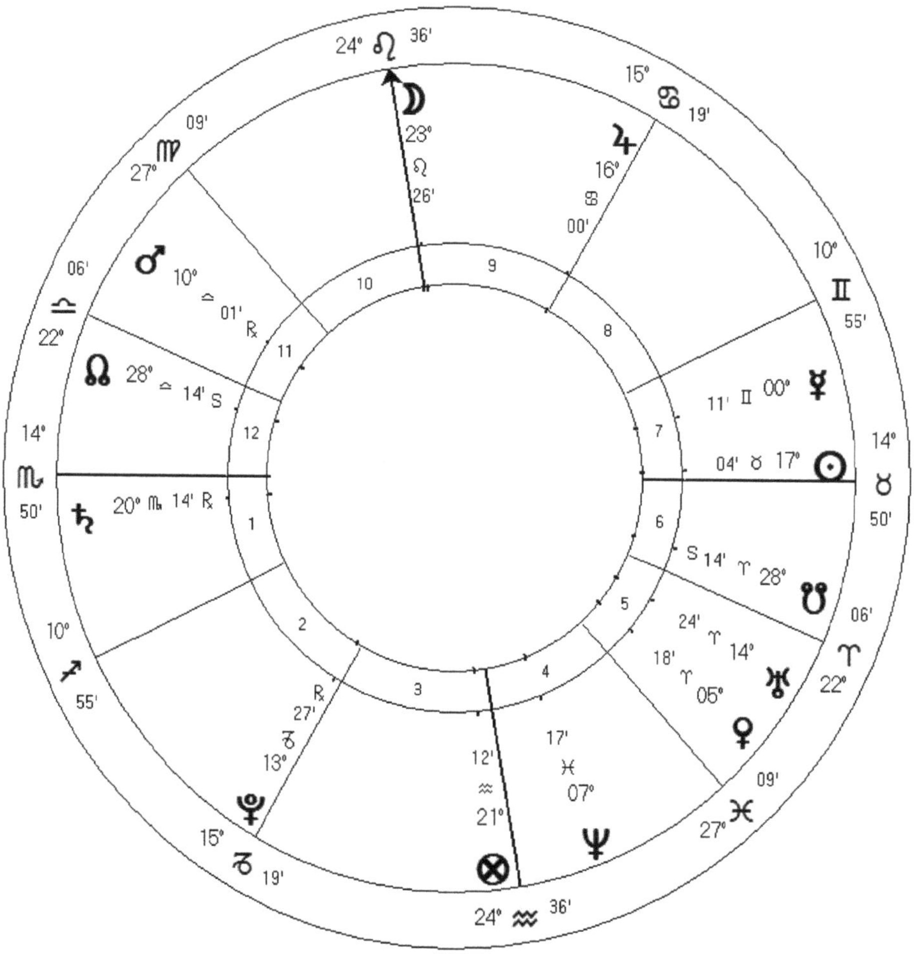

May 07, 2014, 8:14 P.M. | Thessaloniki, Greece | 14 Scorpio

The querent had been expecting the payment for many months as the client's company had suddenly gone under complete restructuring and all financial matters were frozen. She communicated with the client and had been told that the payment would possibly be made in a couple of months. But the situation had initiated fears that the payment would be further delayed or even indefinitely postponed.

The querent's significator is Mars, his cosignificator the Moon. In questions regarding payments an aspect of the client's money with the Lord of the querent's 2nd house – the querent's pockets – can also suffice.

In this case Lord 2 is Jupiter. The client, on the other hand, is signified by Lord 7, which is this case is Venus. However the house of concern here is the 8th representing the client's money (as the 2nd house of the 7th) – signified in this chart by Mercury. So, we would hope to find an applying aspect between one of the querent's significators and the client's money that is represented by Mercury.

We can see that Mercury has just entered its own sign: good news, as this shows that the client's financial situation has very recently improved. There isn't an immediate aspect between the significator at hand. The Moon is currently void of course: this is an indication that the matter should proceed with difficulties. It will, though, aspect (square) Mercury the moment it leaves its current sign and enters Virgo. The Moon is not essentially strong, but it is accidentally strong: it is emphatically located right on an angle, the 10th cusp, the highest part of the chart. So the Moon has power to act on the matter. It shall aspect Mercury in about 8 units of time. In the context the querent has given us choosing months as the slowest unit of time would be plausible but we need to take into account that the Moon is located on an angle: it has the accidental power to act, which means that things may develop faster.

The combination of contradictory indications on timing (slow/fast – the Moon in a slow sign, placement on an angle slow theoretically, but at the same time, indication of fast) pointed to choosing the middle unit which was weeks. So the querent would get paid in about 8 weeks – a timing also plausible within the given context. And so it proved.

Will Investing in This Business Prove Profitable for Me?

Leah Cuperman

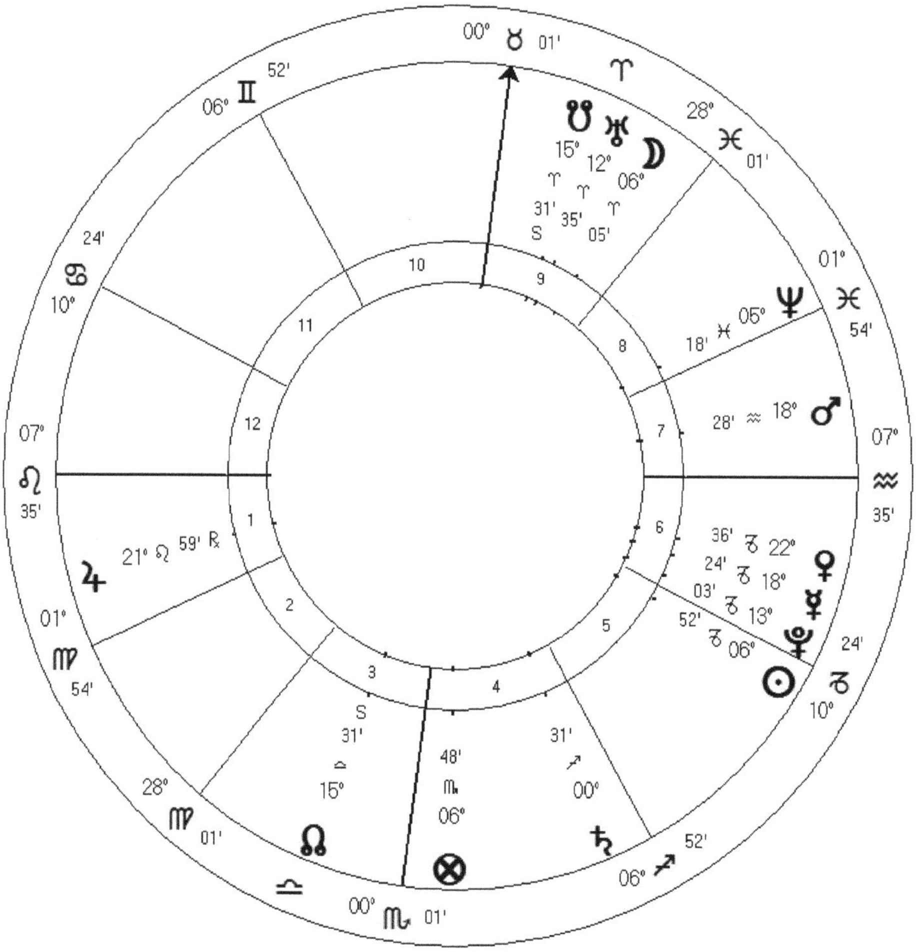

December 28, 2014, 7:04 P.M. | Herzliya, Israel | 7 Leo

The querent was thinking of starting a new business with a partner. The querent's contribution would be somewhat smaller financially, but significant in terms of work and time expended.

He asked: "Will this investment prove profitable for me?"

In this chart, the querent is signified by Lord 1, the Sun, at 6:52 Capricorn and by the Moon at 6:05 Aries. The partner is signified by Lord 7, Saturn, at 0:31 Sagittarius. The business they're planning to start is signified by Lord 10, Venus, at 22:36 Capricorn, and the profit from the business by

Lord 11 (the 2nd house from the 10th, i.e. the business's money) which is Mercury at 18:24 Capricorn.

The first thing to note is that the Sun (our querent), Venus (the business) and Mercury (the profit) are all ruled by Saturn. We would expect Saturn (the partner) to be the dominant figure here, as we know that the querent would be only the junior partner, so this in itself is not a disaster.

Mercury (the profit) is weak and remains weak: it has no essential dignity now and is not going to gain dignity any time soon. Besides this, it is ruled by Saturn, which, being in Sagittarius, takes Mercury into its detriment. This is testimony that the partner harms the profit. There is no implication of anything dishonest in this: only that he won't make the business successful.

Saturn has recently entered Sagittarius, but will soon turn retrograde and go back into Scorpio. Once there, it will take Venus (the business) into its detriment: the partner will harm the business.

It's difficult to delineate the absence of testimony, because there is simply nothing there, but there is no testimony showing either Venus, Mercury, or Saturn bringing any benefit to the Sun. Neither the business, the profit, or the partner benefit our querent in any way.

The advice for the client was not to invest his money in this business, because it will not work out.

A year after the judgement was given, the client told me that because he had decided not to make the investment, his partner chose not to start the business after all. As time passed, it became evident that had they started the business, it would have been much more difficult to turn a profit than they had thought. They found that many potential competitors were in a far more advanced stage of preparation than they were. In such a small market this would have made success most unlikely.

Housing

Will We Be Flooded?

John Frawley

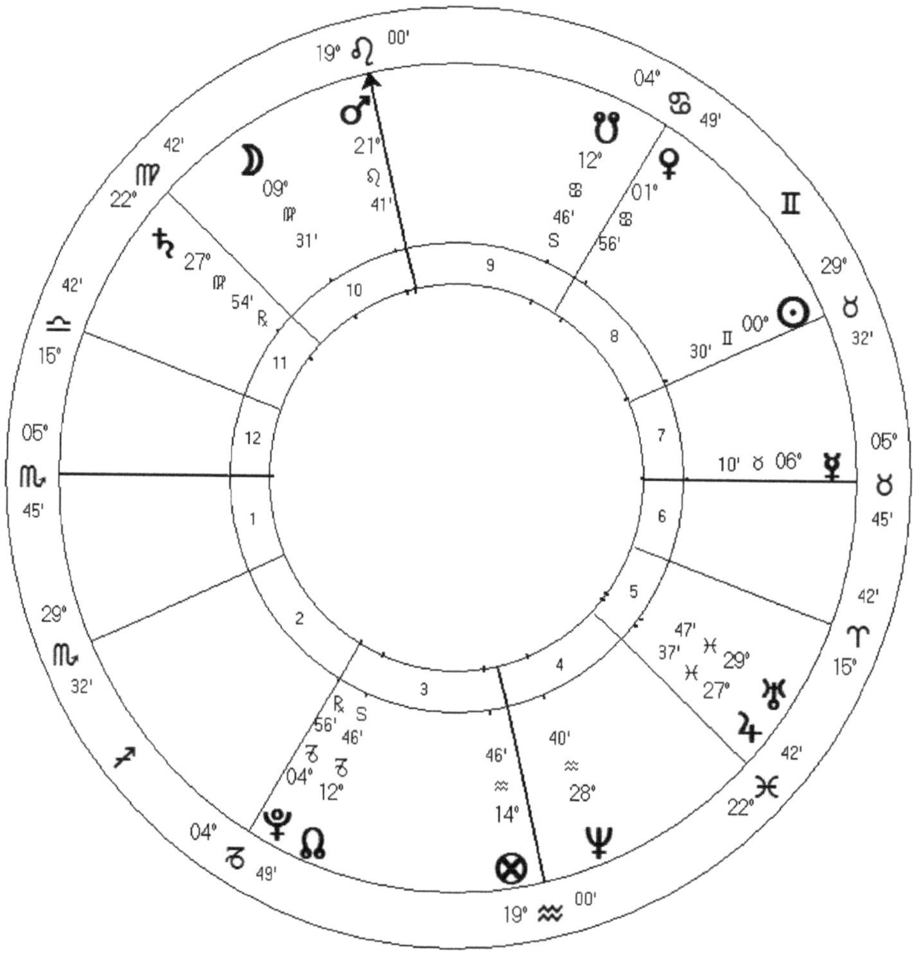

May 21, 2010, 6:05 P.M. | Warsaw, Poland | 5 Scorpio

Amid widespread flooding, the river near my home was coming closer than good manners permit. There had been warnings that the earth embankment separating the house from the river was crumbling.

If I were asking about my house as a piece of real estate, as in "Will he buy my house?" it would be shown by the 4th house of the chart. But that is not the issue here: what concerns me is not a piece of property alien to myself, but the general "here" of the place – my home, the animals, the photos on the walls. As such it is shown by the 1st house, which is, literally, my house.

The 1st house is ruled by Mars, which therefore signifies my home. If I were asking about selling the house it would be necessary to distinguish between me – the person doing the selling – and the house, the thing that is being sold. There is no such need here: I'm not asking if I will be flooded, so I am irrelevant to the question.

Mars is in Leo, a hot/dry sign: nothing wet there. It makes no aspect with anything that might indicate wetness. It is right at the top of the chart: high up, the best place for it to be if the waters are rising. So far, so good. The river, though, might have other ideas.

To identify the river in the chart we need to find something that is wet. Jupiter is the god of rain, which is what the river was full of. It is in Pisces, a watery sign, so it is a very watery god of rain. Jupiter must signify the river. It is near the bottom of the chart, down low, where it belongs. So far, still so good.

But a river in flood rises. Jupiter is doing just that, rising up towards the Descendant as it progresses through the zodiac. As it does this it bumps immediately into Saturn, by opposition. What is Saturn? It's the natural ruler of barriers and is in an earth sign. It must signify the earth embankment, which the waters are about to hit. This exactly pictures the situation.

Reading Saturn as the embankment is confirmed by Mercury. The significant thing about Saturn being in Virgo is Virgo's earthiness. Mercury, the ruler of Virgo, will signify that earthiness. What kind of earthiness? Mercury is in Taurus, so it's a fixed kind of earthiness, appropriate for an embankment. It's right on the Descendant, at the boundary between "down there", where the water is, and "up here", where my house is. We have not only a fixed kind of earthiness, but a "barrier to low stuff rising" kind of earthiness.

So far, the chart has shown nothing that is not already known. The waters will hit the embankment; the question is, will the embankment hold? Saturn is in the detriment of Jupiter, which is a positive sign. Jupiter has no power over it. That's good news. We could read this as it hating Jupiter, in which case it won't wish to cooperate with it. But this is not enough evidence to judge that the embankment will hold. Invaded countries hate their invaders, but this doesn't mean they are able to repel them.

Saturn is close to trine with the Sun. This means it must be near station. Indeed, it is in station. It's not moving. Which is exactly how an embankment should be. This is the crucial testimony, showing that the embankment will hold and the house will not be flooded. And so, I was relieved to find, it proved.

Note: the texts tell us that a planet in station is very weak. This is not so. Whether station shows strength, weakness, or is of no significance depends on what the planet in station signifies. Here, it shows not weakness but strength, for it is in not moving that an embankment's strength is found. Similarly, if I were in the front line I would be delighted to find the planet signifying the soldiers around me in station: if they aren't moving they won't run away.

The same is true of retrogradation: it can be good, bad, or neither, depending upon the context.

Should I Stay Here or Move Back to X?

Molly Morrissey

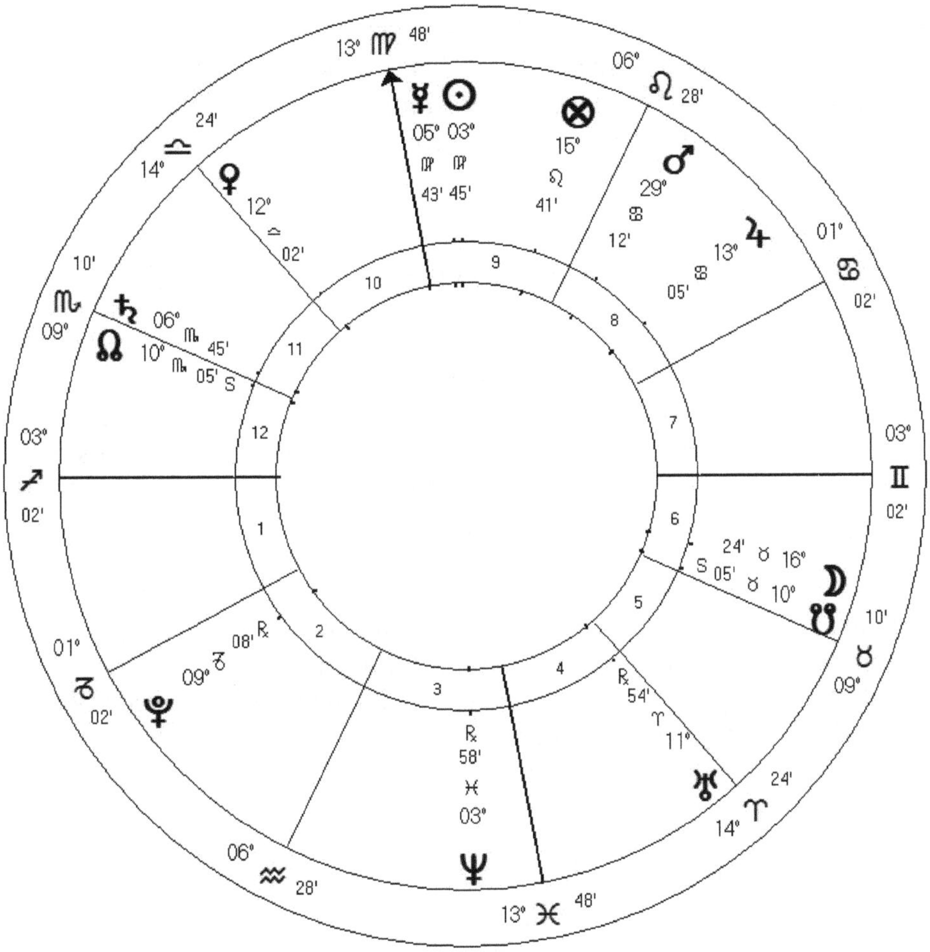

August 26, 2013, 1:28 P.M. | San Diego, CA | 2 Sagittarius

The querent was considering a move back to a city in which she'd lived for a few years prior. She was having a tough time financially and thought she'd be in a better financial situation in the other city.

This is a classic "stay or go?" sort of question where we are comparing the merits of two places against each other. "Here" is always the first house and "there" is given to the opposite place, the seventh house.

The querent gets Lord Ascendant, Jupiter, and the Moon. Jupiter is exalted, confirmation for the querent's reporting that she does really enjoy living where she is. The Moon is also exalted in Taurus: again, a strong placement translating to support her current satisfaction, even if slightly exaggerated.

There are no afflictions to the first house, and the strong Lord 1 is a testimony for staying put. Incidentally, her 2nd house of finances is ruled by a peregrine Saturn, which takes her Moon into fall. Yes, she is disappointed with the state of her bank account. This is the source of the pain that is driving the question.

Looking at the seventh house, the Descendant is afflicted by the antiscion of a weak Mars, in triplicity but also in fall.

Lord 7, Mercury is very strong in its own sign of Virgo, also being in its exaltation. Though being combust the Sun would usually be a strong negative testimony, here it would be taken like a mutual reception, since the Sun is also in Mercury's sign of Virgo. The other location, on its own merits, is a reasonably good place to be, but notice that Mercury in Virgo takes Jupiter into its detriment. It's a very bad place for the querent to be.

The querent is happy where she is, and she's in a good place, even if it's not quite as good as it's made out to be. Going back to the other place would be a very bad idea for the querent. I also pointed out that the querent was disappointed in the state of her finances more than she was upset with her living circumstance. She agreed this was true. The judgment was then for her to stay, and put the focus toward improving the finances.

The querent stayed, put herself onto an austerity plan, and a year later was happy to report that she was really glad she stayed and that she has improved her financial situation quite a bit. She realized that going back wouldn't have been the panacea it seemed.

Will the Bank Foreclose?

Leah Cuperman

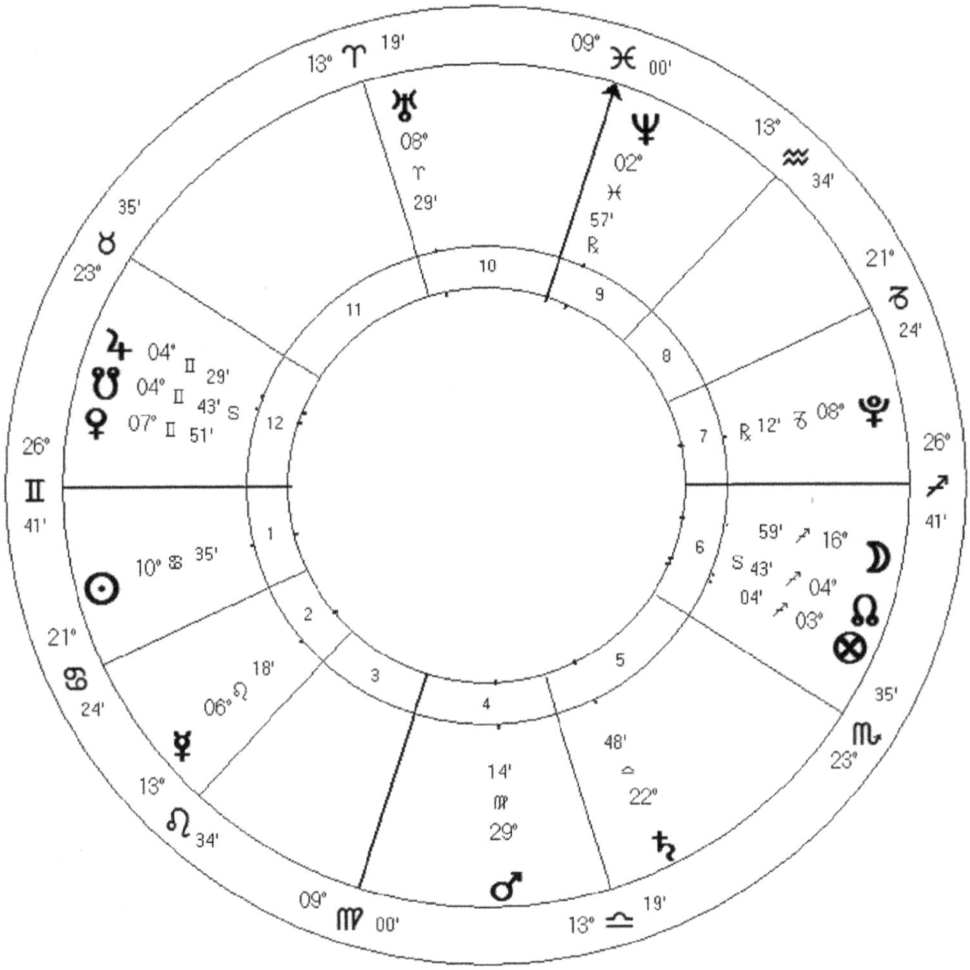

July 02, 2012, 4:41 A.M. | Herzliya, Israel | 26 Gemini

After being unable to pay her mortgage for a few months, the querent had a meeting with the bank, asking them to refinance the debt. She was now waiting for their decision. She asked, "Will the bank approve the refinancing or will they foreclose? Will we have to move out?"

The querent in this chart is signified by Lord 1, Mercury, at 6:18 Leo. The bank, as the people with whom the querent has made a deal, is signified by Lord 7, Jupiter, at 4:29 Gemini. The house too is signified by Mercury, which also rules the 4th house, showing the possessions we cannot move around. There is no problem in having both the querent and the house signified by the same planet, because we don't need an aspect between them in order to answer the question. Mercury is in Leo, a fixed sign. This fixity is strong testimony that the querent will not be moving.

This is a night-time chart (the Sun is below the horizon), so Mercury is in the triplicity of Jupiter. Jupiter, meanwhile, is in the sign, triplicity, and term of Mercury. There is strong mutual reception between the two planets. This argues that the querent and the bank will be able to reach an agreement. Jupiter's conjunction with the South Node, which diminishes or decreases, suggests that the bank will not be flaunting its power by insisting on enforcing its rights. This too argues against foreclosure.

Mercury separates from a sextile aspect to Jupiter. That the aspect is separating shows that something has already happened. This must signify the querent's meeting with the bank. The mutual reception between the two planets shows it went well, and the fact that Mercury is in a fixed sign and is not about to make any significant change shows that the status quo is maintained. We can be sure the bank will agree to refinance, and the querent will be able to stay in her house.

And so it proved.

Should I Move to My Friend's House?

Fotini Christodoulou

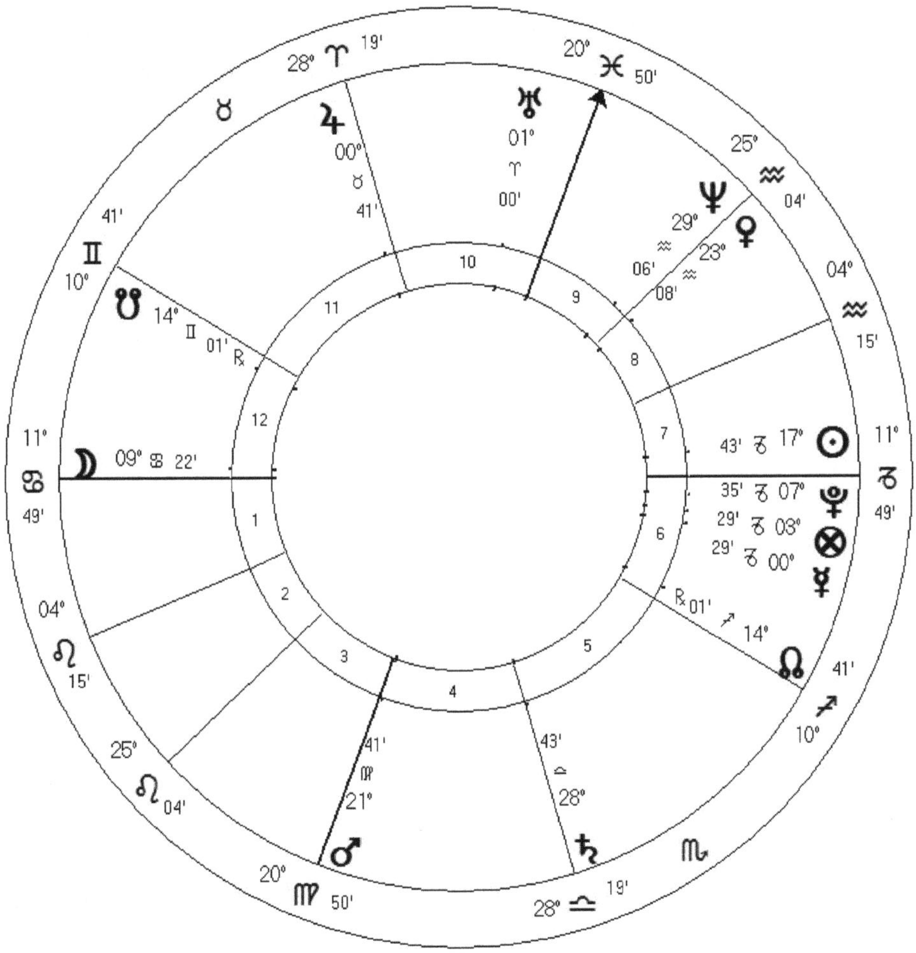

January 08, 2012, 4:44 P.M. | Thessaloniki, Greece | 11 Cancer

The querent's friend was about to move to another country, while the querent was searching to rent a new house. The querent's friend suggested that he'd move into to their house while they are away. The querent was unsure about whether he would be happy in that particular house.

The querent is signified by the Moon, located in the 1st house in Cancer. The friend's house is signified by the 11th, cusp 28:19 degrees of Aries, ruled by Mars. As we can see the querent is not fond of the friend's house (his significator is located in Cancer, Mars' fall). But if we mentally take Lord 1 and place it just inside the 11th house we can see that it'll be at the point of entering its exaltation in Taurus – a very nice place to be after all. So perhaps the querent will feel a bit strange at first but very soon he will feel at home.

The querent moved into that house, and while he had a difficult time adjusting the first few days he was very pleased and happy after he settled in.

When Will the House Get Rented? Will We Need to Hire an Agent?

Molly Morrissey

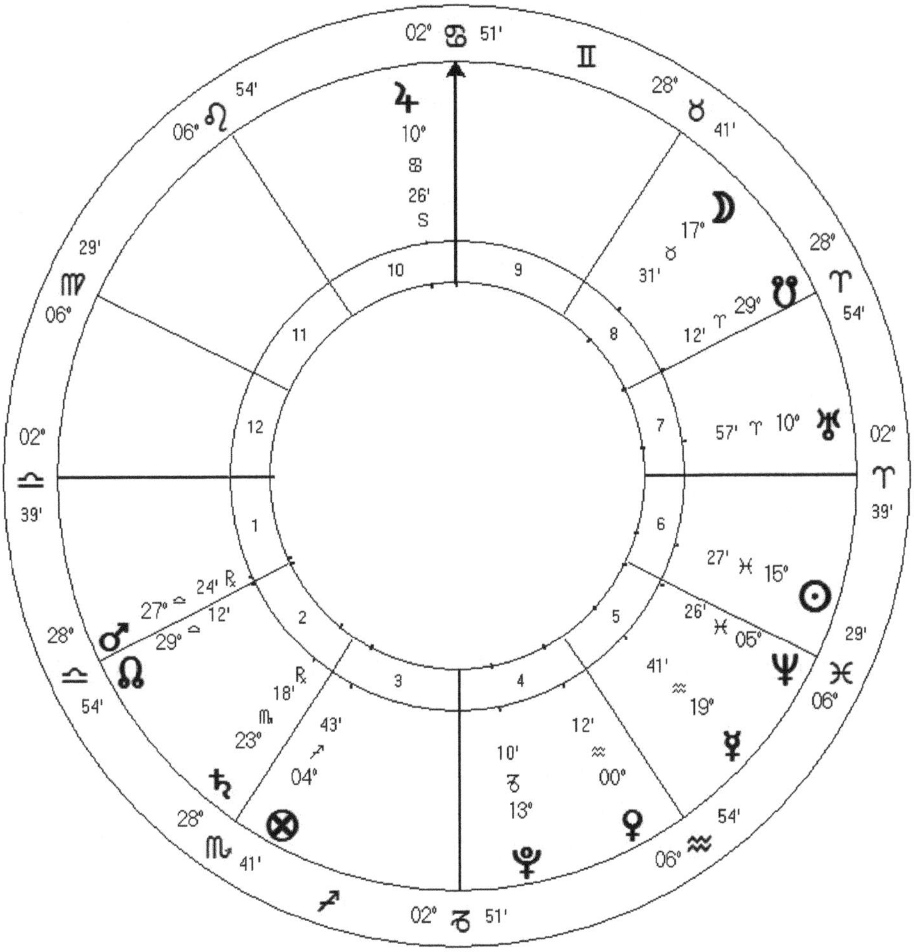

March 05, 2014, 7:06 P.M. | San Diego, CA | 2 Libra

The client's husband was switching jobs and they were to be moving to a different city. They needed to re-rent the house they had been living in to be released from their lease with no penalty. They were hoping to have it taken care of before they left town. They were considering hiring a rental agent to facilitate the process.

This chart is a "When will the deal be done?" sort of chart. They know the house will be re-rented eventually, so it's only a matter of time, and whether someone else will facilitate the transaction.

Because we are mainly looking for timing, we can push planets through prohibitions if an aspect is possible, with the usual constraints of conjunction with the Sun or retrogradation. Luckily, this chart behaves nicely and gives us a trine to work with.

The querent, as usual, gets Lord 1, Venus, and the Moon. The other party, the people who will rent the property, get Lord 7, Mars.

But here we have a subtle issue. The querent was not actually renting the house, though was responsible for getting it re-rented to be released from their lease. In this particular instance, it seemed to me that the querent was one in the same with the actual owners of the house, with whom they were coordinating the re-rental process.

The chart bears this out. Venus is applying to trine Mars. This aspect happens in about 23 degrees.

The only time unit that makes sense here is days. Judgment was that the house would be re-rented by the 28th of March.

Since this trine aspect happened with no collection or translation of light, I took that as testimony that no agent would be necessary.

And so it proved. The querent had confirmation of new renters on the 28th, with a new lease signed with owners on the 29th and without hiring an agent. The transaction was completed before the querent was due to leave town.

Should I Buy This Flat?

Leah Cuperman

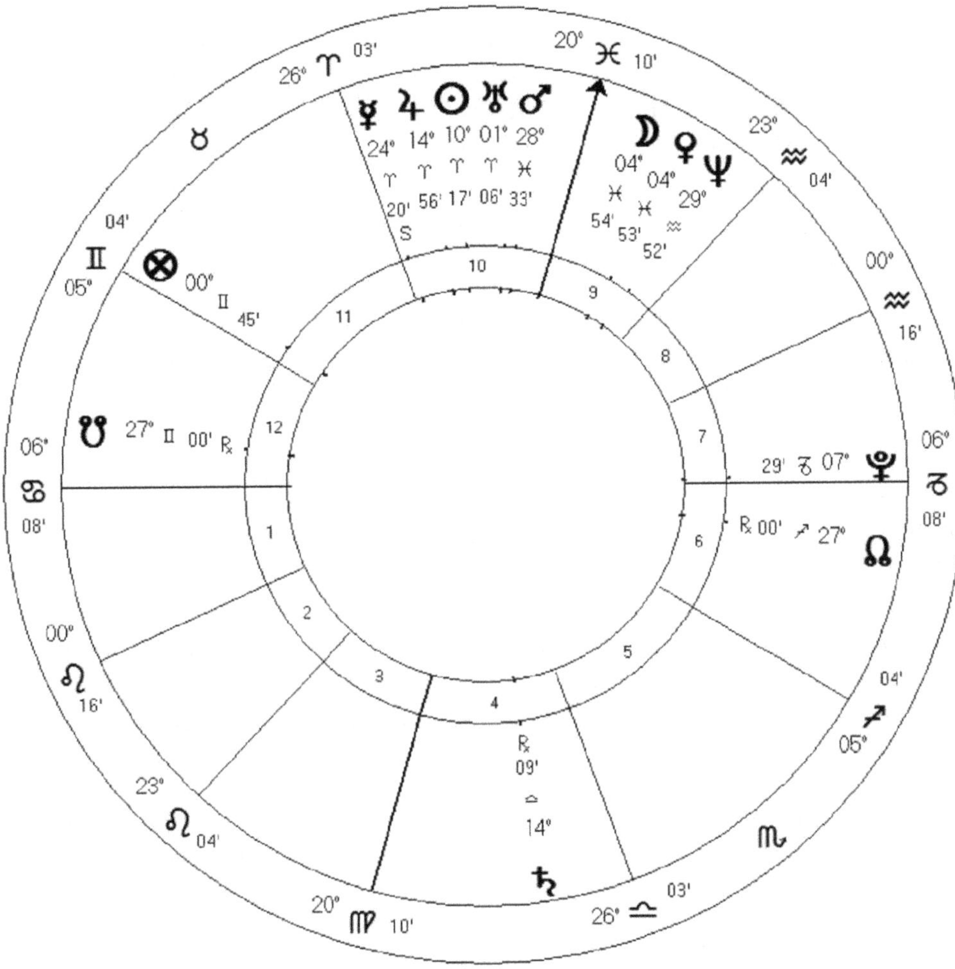

March 31, 2011, 10:31 A.M. | Herzliya, Israel | 6 Cancer

The person asking this question had wanted to buy a flat in a new building the previous year, but the bank wouldn't lend her the money. A year passed by and she realized the flat was still for sale, and at the same low price. Once again, she applied for a loan and this time it was approved. She paid a deposit to hold the flat while she decided if it was the one she wanted to buy.

Her question was: is this flat a good option or should I keep looking?

Even though the client didn't ask what condition the flat was in – probably because it was in a new building – it is important to see what the chart has to tell us about this.

The property – whether the one you're thinking of buying or the one you're planning to sell – is an immovable possession, and thus shown by the radical 4th house. Lord 4 is Mercury. Its condition will tell us about the condition of the property. Mercury at 24:20 Aries is peregrine, which means it has no essential dignity, and it's also retrograde, showing how debilitated it is. This is bad news: the property, even though it's new, is in terrible condition.

If this were an old building the poor condition would not necessarily be a problem: the buyer might be prepared to invest some money in renovating. But this was a building that was only a year old, so this is a red-flag warning.

Let's look now at the price of the property. This is shown by Lord 10, Jupiter at 14:56 Aries. Here, Jupiter not only has no essential dignity (it is peregrine), but being less than 8½ degrees from the Sun and in the same sign, it is also combust: this is the worst thing that can happen to a planet. This not only confirms that the price of the property is low, as the client had told me, but because Jupiter is getting deeper into combustion, the price will decrease even more. If she asks for a price reduction, she can surely get it.

A third important issue to look at when buying a property is the condition of the neighbors: even if the flat were in a palace, nasty neighbors could make life hell. Our neighbors, as the people we encounter in our daily round, are signified by Lord 3. But because we are not talking about the client's current neighbors but the neighbors of the property she's thinking of buying, we need to use the turned 3rd house to locate them: the 3rd from the 4th, the property's neighbors. This is the radical 6th house.

Just like the 10th house, the turned 3rd is signified by Jupiter. But this is not a problem: a planet can have a second role to show us another relevant point in the chart. We saw above that Jupiter not only doesn't have essential dignity, but it is also combust by the rays of the Sun: this shows that the neighbors are dreadful people that the client would wish to avoid at all costs.

We can still dig a bit more to see what the client thinks of the flat, and if the flat will make the client happy. Lord 1, which signifies the client, is the Moon at 4:54 Pisces. There, the Moon is in the rulership of Jupiter, but being in the opposite house of the 4th also puts it in the detriment and fall of Mercury, which signifies the flat. This tells us that the client is in love with the price of the flat, but strongly dislikes the flat itself. What does the flat think about the client? Mercury at 24:20 Aries is in no dignity of the Moon, the client. Just as there are places that make us feel welcome and comfortable, this flat is totally indifferent and couldn't care less about her.

Another point of importance is the immediate opposition by antiscion between Lord 1 (the Moon) and Lord 4 (Mercury): Lilly (see Glossary) says that opposition brings things together with regret. If the client decides to buy the flat after all, she will regret it.

My advice to the client was to reconsider the purchase of this property.

I told her it was in terrible condition, deteriorating; that the neighbors were not people she would like to live close to; and that even though the price could be reduced, she should think twice before going ahead.

The client was surprised, as she told me it was hard to believe the flat was already in bad condition and deteriorating when the building was only one year old and no one had lived in the flat yet.

Two days later, I received an email from her. She had gone to see the flat again, and met a person who was living in the same building.

This person told her about all the problems she had with her flat: the poor quality of the building materials that had been used; a problem with the gas that would cost a lot to have fixed; frequent problems with the electricity and unusually high bills; and, yes, noisy and inconsiderate neighbors.

She was happy that she could get her deposit back and cancel the purchase.

Will We Rent the House?

Molly Morrissey

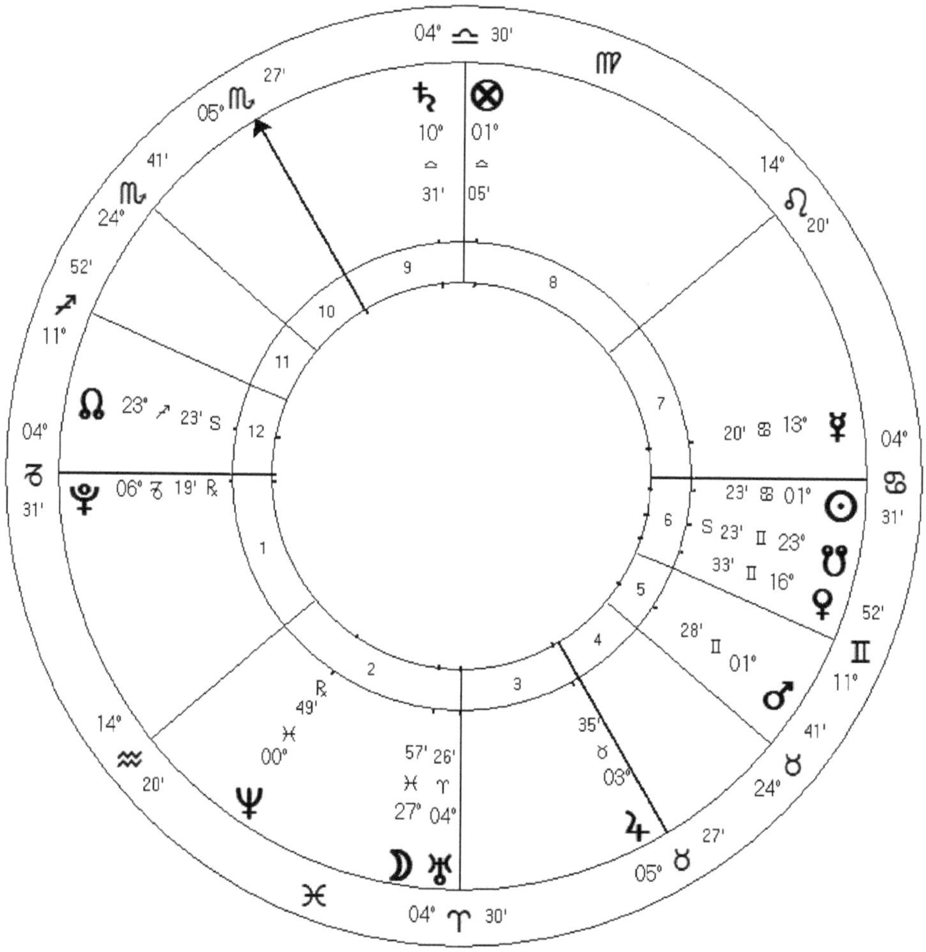

June 22, 2011, 9:18 P.M. | Seattle, WA | 4 Capricorn

We were moving to New Mexico in several weeks' time and one rental house had already fallen through. Another house had become available and we wanted to rent it, but a sale on the house had to be finalized before we could sign the lease with the new owners through a property manager. At the time the question was asked, we had seen the house and had told them we wanted it. We had also been previously approved by the property manager during the rental process that had fallen through. All we needed was the sale to go through. Because of the short time frame, I was anxious for the deal to be done.

Since this is a “Will the deal be done?” sort of question, the querent (me) is signified by Lord 1, Saturn. The house owner gets Lord 7, the Moon. The querent typically would also get the Moon, though in this case the Moon is taken as major signifier for another relevant party.

The Moon is just about to change sign. This indicates that the Moon is the significator for the current owner who is selling the house – not the people that we would rent from.

In looking for the new owners’ significator, I noticed the antiscion of Lord 4, Venus (the property) is conjunct Mercury, who is sitting in the 7th house. When looking for another significator, using another planet sitting in the appropriate house is valid. The conjunction by antiscion confirms the use of Mercury as significator of the new owners, which also confirms the sale going though.

Mercury is separating from an aspect with Lord Ascendant, Saturn. This confirms that the deal has already been done.

And so it proved. The sale closed only days before our stuff and I got there, and we moved in with ease. Indeed, the deal had already been done.

Relationship

Will the Relationship Last?

Fotini Christodoulou

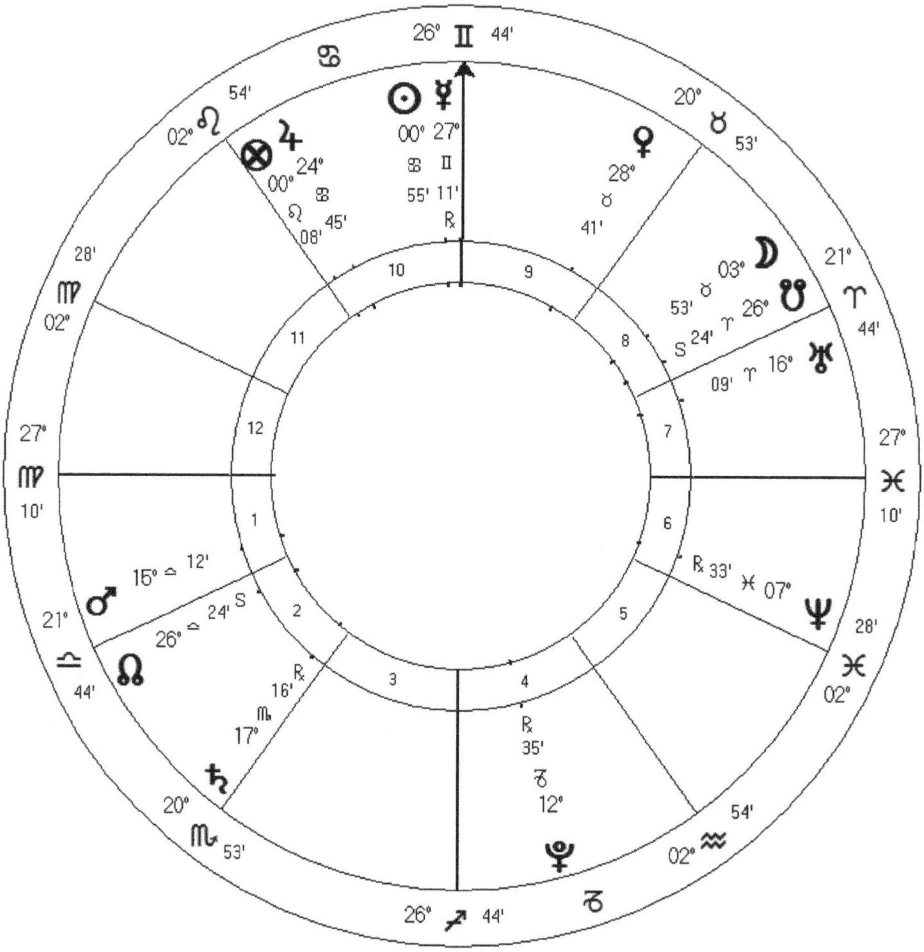

June 22, 2014, 1:12 P.M. | Thessaloniki, Greece | 27 Virgo

The querent was having a relationship which at some point had become long-distanced as her boyfriend had moved to another country. After a few months they had agreed that she would also move there so that they would live together. But as the time for the move was approaching she started having second thoughts about the matter, worrying if the relationship would last.

In any question concerning relationship matters besides the obvious significators that are Lord 1 and the Moon for the querent and Lord 7 for the partner, we also give Venus to the woman and the Sun to the man. Lords 1 and 7 will show us what the people involved feel/think about each other as "heads" / personalities. The Moon will show us what the querent's heart wants. Venus and the Sun will show us what they want on a more physical level, to their roles as woman and man.

In this case Lord 1 is Mercury: in a perfect square to the Ascendant/Descendant axis, symbolically torn between herself and her boyfriend, accurately showing her perplexed mental state. We can see that Mercury is in retrograde motion and has recently re-entered its own sign. It was in the exaltation of Lord 7 (Cancer), thinking very highly of her boyfriend but re-entering her own sign (the boyfriend's detriment) is showing that she was expecting too much of him and consequently was disappointed in him, or that she had a priority change: in the very recent past her only priority had been the boyfriend, but now she is thinking of herself and what she wants, first. So far, we see how she started having second thoughts.

Her heart, the Moon, is located in its exaltation (Taurus) and ruled by her woman-side (Venus): she wants some serious emotional attention and reassurance as a woman. Venus in the same sign, with lots of dignity indicates the same needs, but as those two are in a mutual reception, they come with a serious degree of self-involvement. This matches exactly the querent's mental state: thinking what she wants, and about her own priorities.

Furthermore the placement of Lord 1 on the 10th cusp along with the amount of interest on her Venus side, which is at the moment strong, show us how important the fact of providing for herself is for her. Indeed the querent admitted that she was stressed about leaving her steady job, moving and not being able to provide for herself at least at the start and that she would be depending on her boyfriend. She believed that he was not enough interested in the relationship.

The boyfriend's significators are Jupiter, Lord 7, and the Sun, both located in Cancer: ruled by her heart. Jupiter in its exaltation may show someone who thinks highly of himself, perhaps over estimating his abilities. The Sun, has just entered Cancer: he was until now attracted to her as a person, but now is ruled by her heart and exalting himself. There is an amount of self-interest here too, but with a different dynamic: he believes he has the power to act to win her heart and to make this work. Can he deliver? Jupiter with lots of essential dignity and also in the 10th – he can. Why then is she feeling so unsure about the way he sees their relationship? Both his significators, the Sun and Jupiter, are located in a Mute sign: he's not communicating his interest appropriately.

The relationship itself is shown by the Part of Marriage which in this case is located at 25:40 degrees of Cancer so its dispositor in this chart is the Moon. The Moon, as mentioned, is located in Taurus: it has a lot of essential dignity and also is in a fixed sign. That shows a happy and long-lasting relationship. We have also found that both the boyfriend's significators are in Cancer, showing that he highly values their relationship and all the more as Jupiter falls on the Part itself, strong essentially, that he can help make this work. The querent is obviously also interested in it, but as this placement shows, she is the one that rules it (the Moon). We can also see her woman-side is thinking very highly of the relationship now, but as Venus will soon change sign, and start being ruled by her head (what her head – Mercury – wants), her priorities as a woman will change.

As in many relationship questions, the untangling of the querent's and partner's thoughts and emotions, is the answer itself: Horary can be used as a very insightful consultative tool. The direct judgment to the question was that this relationship can and will last, if she wants it to. As the boyfriend's significators were silent (Cancer) it was proposed that she would talk about her insecurities and stresses to him. So she did and the situation was resolved. The querent happily moved in with her boyfriend. However the stresses as indicated by the chart remain in effect.

Will I Be Any Happier If I Leave Him?

Kathryn Silvestre

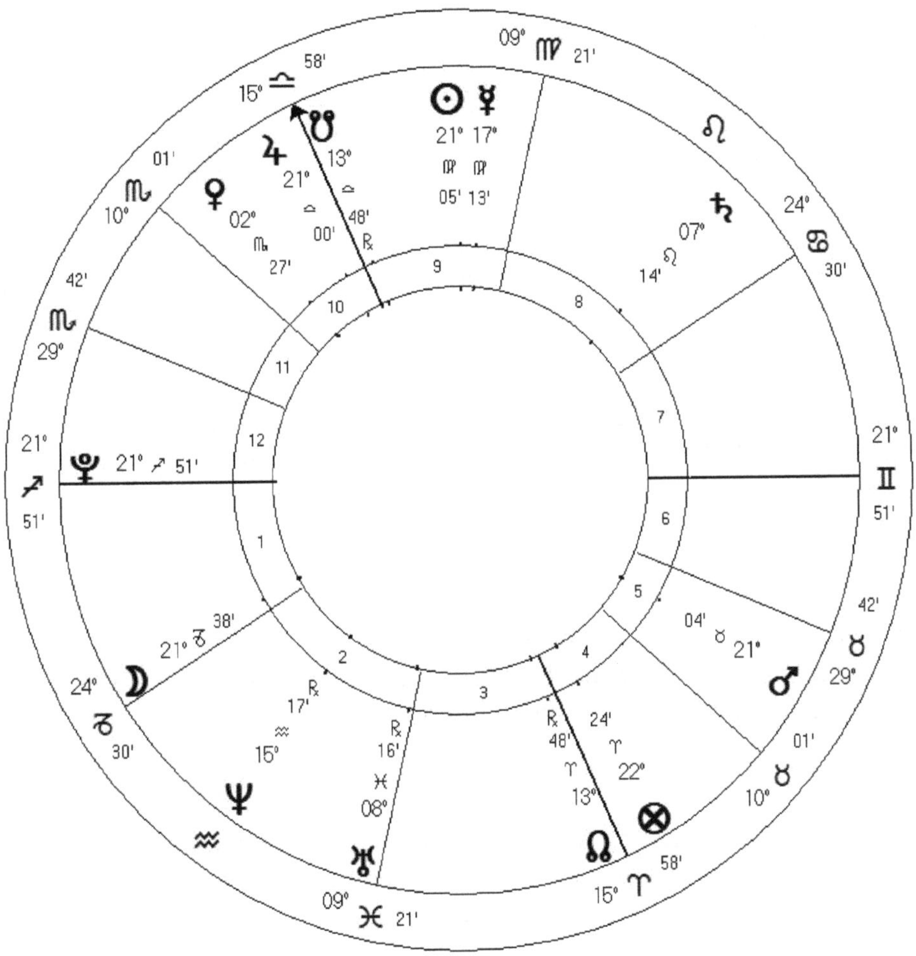

September 13, 2005, 2:19 P.M. | Milwaukee, WI | 21 Sagittarius

The querent was unhappy in her marriage but conflicted about making any changes. She'd used horary before and was hoping the consultation might help her move in one direction or the other. She was worried about the consequences of divorcing and feared things might be no better for her if she left, as her phrasing of the question shows.

The first thing to note here is that the question, as worded, cannot really be answered. Essentially this is a "What if?" question. But we cannot look at "what if" in horary, only at "what is." The querent hasn't left her husband, nor has she decided to leave him. But she is seeking guidance, which horary can certainly provide. Relationship horaries spell out just how two people are feeling about each other and, using the Part of Marriage, we can also see how the relationship itself is faring.

First, let's identify the players.

Sagittarius rises, so our querent is signified by Jupiter, ruler of Sagittarius. Jupiter is our querent as head. She is also assigned the Moon, signifying her heart, and Venus, signifying her as woman. The querent's husband is assigned Mercury (ruler of Gemini) as Lord 7 and the Sun as natural ruler of him as man. The Sun plays a second important role in this chart as dispositor of the Part of Marriage. Often in relationship questions there is a third party involved in the situation, and so we must ask about this. To my knowledge, there was no third person directly involved here.

Among the first things the reader may notice about this chart is the exact conjunction of Pluto on the Ascendant – exact to the minute of arc! In traditional astrology we treat the outer planets as we do fixed stars, including them if they are conjunct an important planet or point, and taking their meaning from the corresponding myth. Pluto is the god who emerges once from the underworld to snatch the maiden Persephone and carry her home with him. I like to think of Pluto as "something hellish," though one must always consider the context. Here it fits, as the querent felt captive in an unhappy, no-win situation.

Let's look at each of the querent's significators separately, to start.

Jupiter is in Libra: ruled by Venus, the querent as woman, and in the fall of the Sun, her husband as man. Fall in the context of relationships can be understood as either disappointment or loathing – or perhaps both. Jupiter is in the detriment of Mars, the natural ruler of divorce. This part of our querent does not want to leave her husband. Her role as wife is important to her. Any woman considering divorce must consider the consequences, which include material and financial support, companionship, and intimacy.

The Moon in Capricorn is in its own detriment: she is sad. The Moon exalts Mars, natural ruler of divorce, showing us that the querent idealizes divorce as the solution to her troubles. Notice that the Moon is near the cusp of the second house, her finances. The querent hadn't worked outside the home in many years and was reluctant to give up the comfortable living her husband provided. She also had extensive community involvements which were possible only with the freedom that being a homemaker allowed her.

It's important to note that the Moon and Jupiter are in square here, showing the querent's tension and inner conflict. At the same time, they both love Saturn. The financial considerations are very important to our querent!

Venus is in its own detriment in Scorpio, and in the fall of the Moon as well. As wife and love-partner, the querent is unhappy, in a fixed kind of way; and she hates, or is disappointed in, herself emotionally. Being in the sign of Mars, Venus too is interested in, or preoccupied with, the question of divorce.

Taking all three of our querent's significators as a whole we note that only Jupiter has any direct feelings about her husband, and these are negative. Venus and the Moon show no interest by reception in either the Sun or Mercury. The querent's focus in asking the question is herself. There's no love left in the equation for her.

Before we continue the analysis with a look at her husband's significators, it's important to say a few words about Mars here. Mars is in Taurus, ruled by Venus and exalting the Moon. It is also trine both the Sun and the Moon. I don't think it's correct to ascribe any meaning to these mutual receptions or aspects, however. Mars' involvement shows us that divorce is very much on the table in this relationship, as if it were a third party.

Now let's consider the husband's significators, Mercury and the Sun.

Mercury is in Virgo, which it rules and in which it is exalted: the husband is interested in himself. Furthermore, he hates his wife as Jupiter and is disappointed in, and/or loathes, his wife as Venus. The husband does have some positive feelings, too: Virgo is in the triplicity of Venus. But as fall carries more weight than triplicity, the negative feelings predominate. He has no feelings either way for his wife as the Moon. The Sun is also in Virgo, so the same dynamics apply.

Note that although the husband's feelings for his wife are largely negative, he's still very much involved with her. Mixed or negative feelings are preferable to indifference. The husband feels some indifference to our querent as an emotional being, but overall he feels less indifference to her than she does to him. Two of the querent's three significators show no feelings at all for her husband.

Notice how the Sun supports Mercury. Technically speaking Mercury is combust in this chart, but a planet combust in its own sign is enhanced rather than destroyed. Notice, too, the contrast in how the querent feels about herself compared to how her husband feels about himself. She has negative self-feelings, but his are strongly positive.

Now let's look at the Sun in its role as dispositor of the Part of Marriage. To calculate the POM we use the formula of Ascendant + Descendant – Venus. This gives us 131:15 degrees, which converts to 11:15 Leo; the Sun rules Leo, so the Sun signifies the marriage. Read the paragraph just above this one again, this time thinking of the Sun as the marriage. Who has power in the marriage? The husband does. Who benefits? The husband does. Who is harmed? The querent is.

Let's summarize, then. We couldn't tell the querent whether she would be happier leaving her husband, because she hadn't left him. But we did point out how unhappy she was at that time, sharing the insights this horary offers. Although none of this was a surprise to the querent, she continued in the marriage for some years until she discovered her husband intended to harm her with changes to his will. They are now divorced.

Any Chance of a Romance with X?

Kathryn Silvestre

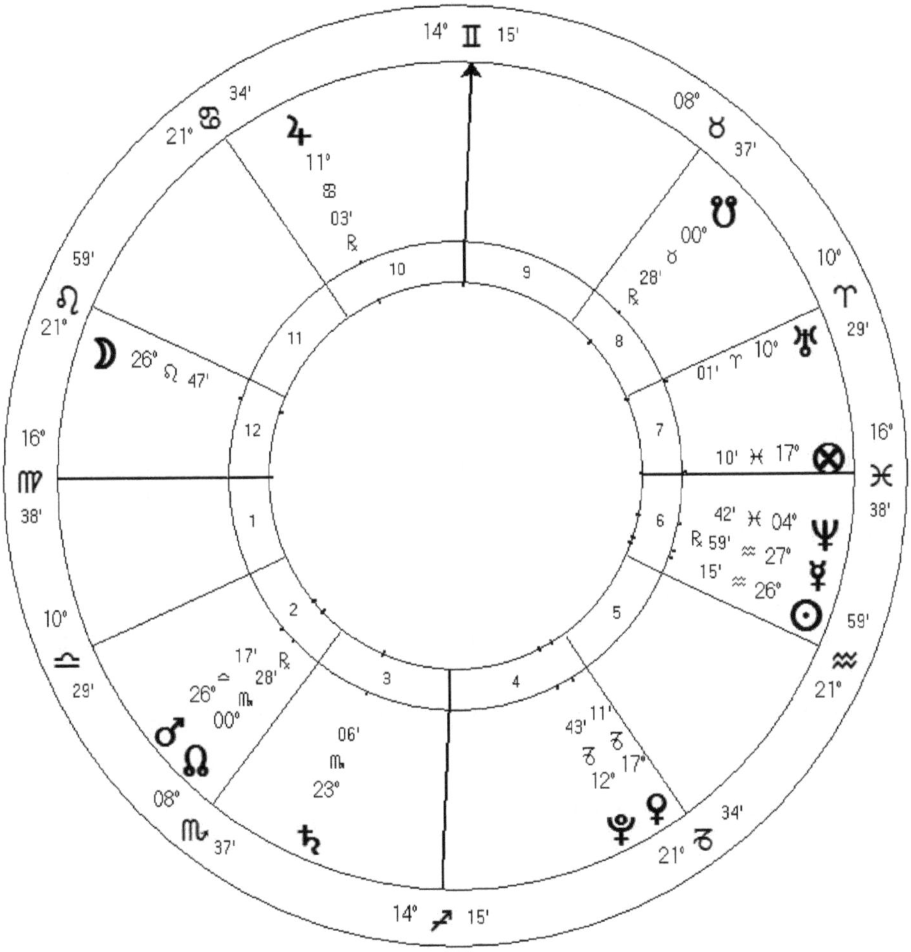

February 14, 2014, 7:03 P.M. | Highland Park, IL | 16 Virgo

Here's a relationship horary from one of my students. Although it's her own question, the judgment is mine, as she is in the early stages of learning horary.

At the time she asked this question, the querent had just enjoyed a first date with a love-interest from her workplace. There had been sparks between them for a long time. He was in the final stages of a divorce; the querent had no other relationship at the time.

In this chart the querent is signified by three planets: Mercury, ruler of Virgo on the Ascendant, for her as thinking person or "head"; the Moon, for her as "heart"; Venus, for her as a woman. Her love interest is signified by Jupiter, ruler of Pisces on the Descendant, and the Sun, for him as a man.

The querent's heart loves her workmate as a man (the Moon is in the Sun's sign of Leo). However, the Moon and the Sun have just separated from opposition, a troubling testimony. Oppositions generally are difficult: stuff happens, but with regret.

The querent as "head" (Mercury) is combusted by the quesited as a man (the Sun in detriment). Ouch! Being in detriment means either he hates himself or he is a Bad Boy, or both. This was a major warning to the querent. But her head and her heart were in direct conflict with each other (opposition). In fact, the querent knew some things about the quesited that were very concerning, but her heart still wanted him. Adding to the complexity of her feelings, as a woman she is disappointed in him (Venus is in the fall of Jupiter).

The quesited as Jupiter is in his own exaltation: as a thinking person, he has a high opinion of himself. Being in Cancer, he also loves the querent's heart, the part of her that admires him. He likes the emotional stuff that he gets from her! However, he has no feelings at all for her as a thinking person or as a woman.

Note that whether the quesited is hating himself (as the Sun in detriment) or exalting himself (as Jupiter in Cancer), he is self-absorbed.

Do these two get together and enjoy a romance? Mercury and the Sun perfect their conjunction, showing that they do enter a relationship. But their affair was relatively brief. After a few months he faded away, "ghosting" her. Because there was no communication from him ending their relationship, for a long time she hung onto the idea that they still had something going between them. In the end, this left the querent feeling used and abused

What in the chart shows this harm to the querent? The Part of Marriage (Ascendant + Descendant - Venus) is 16:05 Scorpio, making Mars the significator of their relationship. Mars is in detriment but on the verge of gaining major essential dignity. This is puzzling at first; Mars in detriment makes sense, in that the relationship was miserable overall. But what about this change that Mars is about to undergo?

Normally we would think of such a gain in essential dignity as a big improvement. Here, however, once Mars (the relationship) enters Scorpio it takes Venus (the querent as woman) into detriment and the Moon (the querent's heart) into fall. This drop in condition by reception certainly reflects what she experienced. The querent is now in the middle stages of recuperation from a relationship that took away much more than it gave.

Is There Any Hope for Us Getting Back Together? Should I Wait for Her?

Fotini Christodoulou

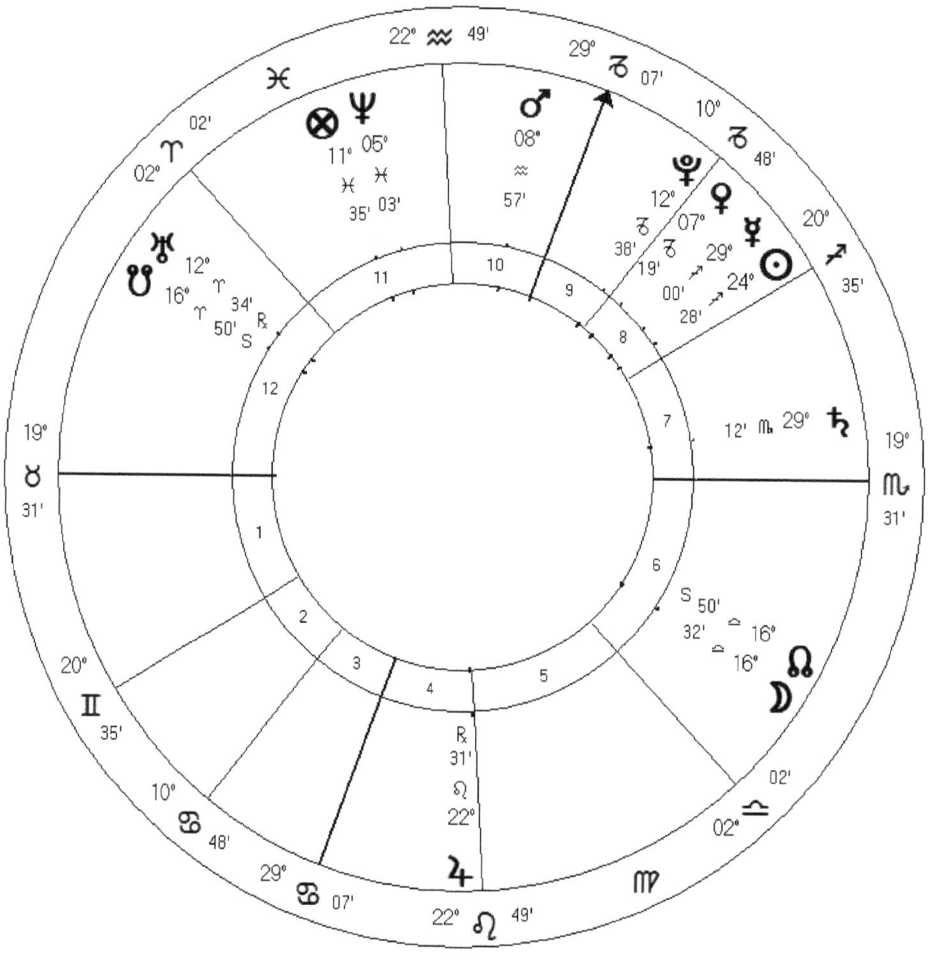

December 16, 2014, 2:53 P.M. | Thessaloniki, Greece | 19 Taurus

The querent is a man asking about a woman with whom he had a lifelong friendship which at some point had turned into a romantic relationship. The woman had broken up with him after a few months because she felt that he wasn't interested in her and went back to her previous boyfriend. The querent had made a few unsuccessful attempts to win her back.

The querent as a personality (as the "head") is signified by Lord 1, Venus. Thc Moon, his cosignificator, is the indicator of his feelings/his heart. As he is a man, the Sun will show what his manly side wants. The quesited, the woman he's inquiring after, is signified in this chart only by Mars.

While the question is about the other person's feelings, we cannot jump straight to that matter, because this has to do with a relationship; it takes two to tango and we must know if they are both inclined to dance and what their motives are towards each other in the first place.

Venus, his head, is located in Capricorn, so he is in the exaltation of Lord 7, Mars (the woman). But he's known this woman since childhood and they had a romantic relationship for months. In this context, the exaltation can only mean that he has idolized her and he expects too much of her. That can only lead to disappointment. Perhaps, as he's been attached to her for many years, he has somehow come to consider her as the "ideal" woman – and no one can live up to that. Venus is also located in Saturn's sign, the Moon's detriment: what his head wants is harming or disappointing him emotionally.

The Moon, as the querent's heart, is located in Libra – it is ruled by his head (Venus), which, as mentioned, is taking it into detriment and it is in Lord 7's (Mars) detriment: his heart is disappointed in this woman. It has just entered the via combusta which is an indicator of serious emotional turmoil and on the North Node, being very emotional (as the North Node expands) and his need for emotional fulfillment much emphasized.

So far we have seen that he has idolized Lord 7, and that what he wants as a head is bringing disappointment to his heart.

His last significator, the Sun, doesn't show any important interest to Lord 7, as it is located in Sagittarius: his manly side is interested in Jupiter with which he is in a very strong mutual reception and also met in the very recent past (it has a separating aspect). So it seems that he has someone else too, even if he sees that person only as a lover – note that, Venus, his head, is in Jupiter's fall.

Lord 7, Mars, is located in Aquarius, and she has a very small interest in Venus (Lord 1). Mars is ruled by Saturn – and as we have seen Lord 1 and the Moon were also in major dignities of Saturn, and all that – in this context – point that Saturn signifies her boyfriend. This is further supported by the fact that her significator, Mars, is in a very strong mutual reception with Saturn. At the same time she's at the Sun's detriment: here the disappointment she had in our querent, which as it proves was generated by his lack of interest in her as a man.

The Part of Marriage is in Aries, so its dispositor Mars is in Aquarius: taking his manly side into detriment (it is a source of disappointment for him as a man) while his head is exalting this relationship (Mars) and his heart is disappointed in it, because it doesn't receive the attention it needs. So overall this relationship is not a good idea for the querent. Lord 7 rules this relationship and its future lies in what she wants. She's not interested, though, as we've seen, and even despite the fact that Saturn is soon to break the reception with her – perhaps her boyfriend will break up with her – her significator is in a fixed sign and will continue to want Saturn and be disappointed in our querent's manly side.

The querent confirmed the above. As in most cases the resolution in this type of questions usually comes from untangling the querent's feelings and the situation as it is; and so it did in this case.

Will She Talk to Me Again? Am I Important to Her?

Marcos Monteiro

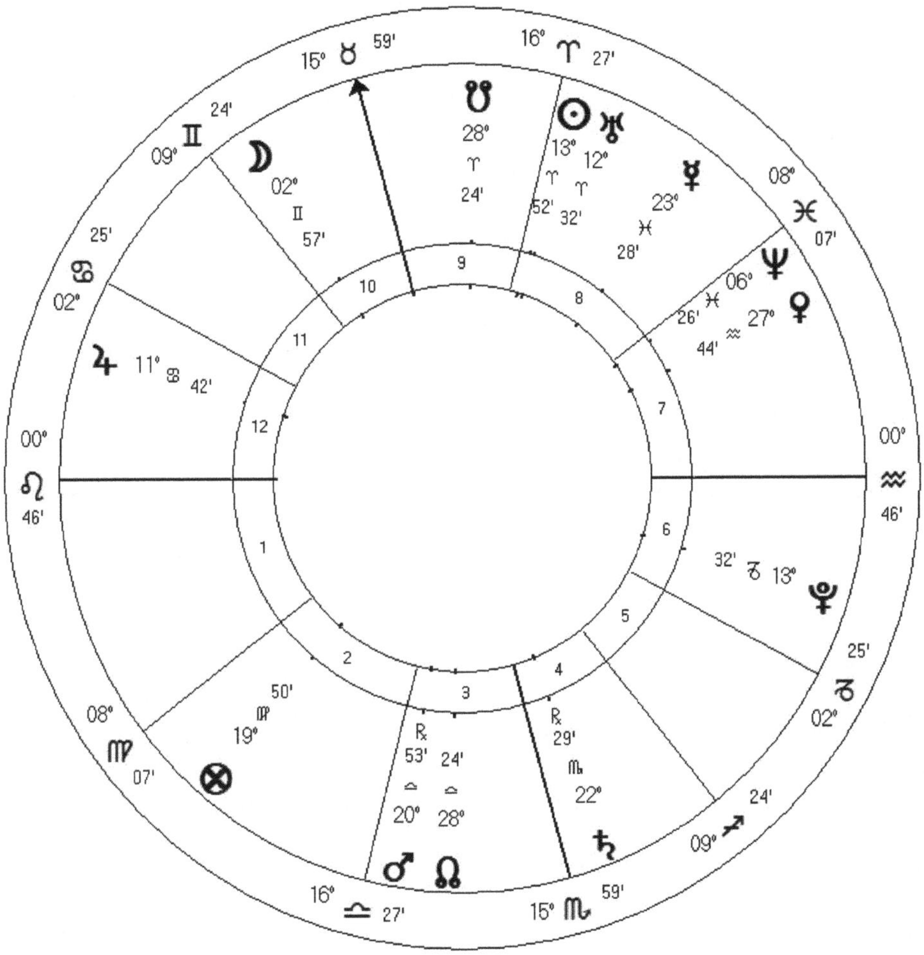

April 03, 2014, 2:21 P.M. | Barra Velha/SC, Brazil | 0 Leo

The querent had a student with whom he had, according to him, a very intense relationship for a couple of months. He had asked her to marry him; she hadn't answered.

Sometime later they had a discussion. She thought he was harassing her and told him to leave her alone, and never talk to him again. So, the querent wanted to know a) if she would talk to him again, b) if he was still important to her, and c) if she thought of marrying him.

The querent, as the person asking the question, gets the lord of the 1st house, the Sun, and the Moon (cosignificator or the querent).

The lady about whom he asked the question gets the lord of the 7th, Saturn, and Venus, natural ruler of women in relationship issues.

First, it's noteworthy that the Sun, our querent, is in Aries. The Sun has its exaltation there, but it's also Saturn's fall and Venus's detriment. It may seem odd, but not every love question is asked out of pure love.

The Sun in Aries exalts itself. The querent lifts himself up – he thinks highly of himself. At the same time, it's in Saturn's fall – he is disappointed in her, she hurt his feelings (or his pride) – and in the detriment of Venus. Both planets mean the lady, but Saturn is her as a whole person, or as "head"; Venus is her as female, her sexual drive included. They were not seeing each other for about a year when the question was asked, and she had told her to leave him alone. He didn't like what her Venus was doing at the moment, and the chart emphasizes that.

The Moon reinforces this: it has just left Taurus, a Venus sign, where it loved Venus. Taurus is also the Moon's exaltation, a place where the Moon was very happy. Our querent would like very much to have things as they were before.

A final touch to the situation is that the Sun is conjunct Uranus. Among the few significations we can ascribe to Uranus, "divorce and separation" is one that keeps appearing over and over in relationship charts.

OK, his significators satisfactorily describe the situation. What about hers?

Saturn is in Scorpio. It's in the fall of the Moon (it is disappointed with the Moon, or doesn't like it) and in the detriment of Venus. Does she hate herself? Not necessarily. It may indicate a lot of things: low self-esteem, for example. But we don't know for sure, and it's always best not to include unnecessary assumptions. The woman is not happy with the client's feelings, and not happy with her own female self, so to speak. Saturn is in a fixed sign and retrograde, going further back into Scorpio – this disposition is not likely to change.

Venus is in Aquarius. It's the sign of Saturn, but, more important to our question, it's the detriment of the Sun. This part of her hates the querent, and it has been like that for a while now – Venus is at the end of the sign. Venus is about to change, but nothing will improve for our querent – in the next sign Venus will exalt itself, but will in no way start liking either the Moon or the Sun.

Saturn's in a mute sign, Venus is going from a low-voiced sign into a mute one; neither of them aspects either the Sun or the Moon, so, no, she's not going to talk to him again.

Saturn still loathes the Moon or is disappointed in it; Venus hates the Sun. So the querent is still important to her – although not in the way he would like to be.

Neither of her significators like any of his significators, and the situation is not likely to improve. So, no, she is not thinking of marrying him, and is unlikely to change her mind.

It's common practice to calculate the Part of Marriage (Ascendant + Descendant – Venus) in relationship horaries. I didn't include it in my judgment because they didn't have a relationship anymore.

The situation, as far as I know, hasn't changed from what it was when the question was asked.

Will I Find a New Relationship and When?

Fotini Christodoulou

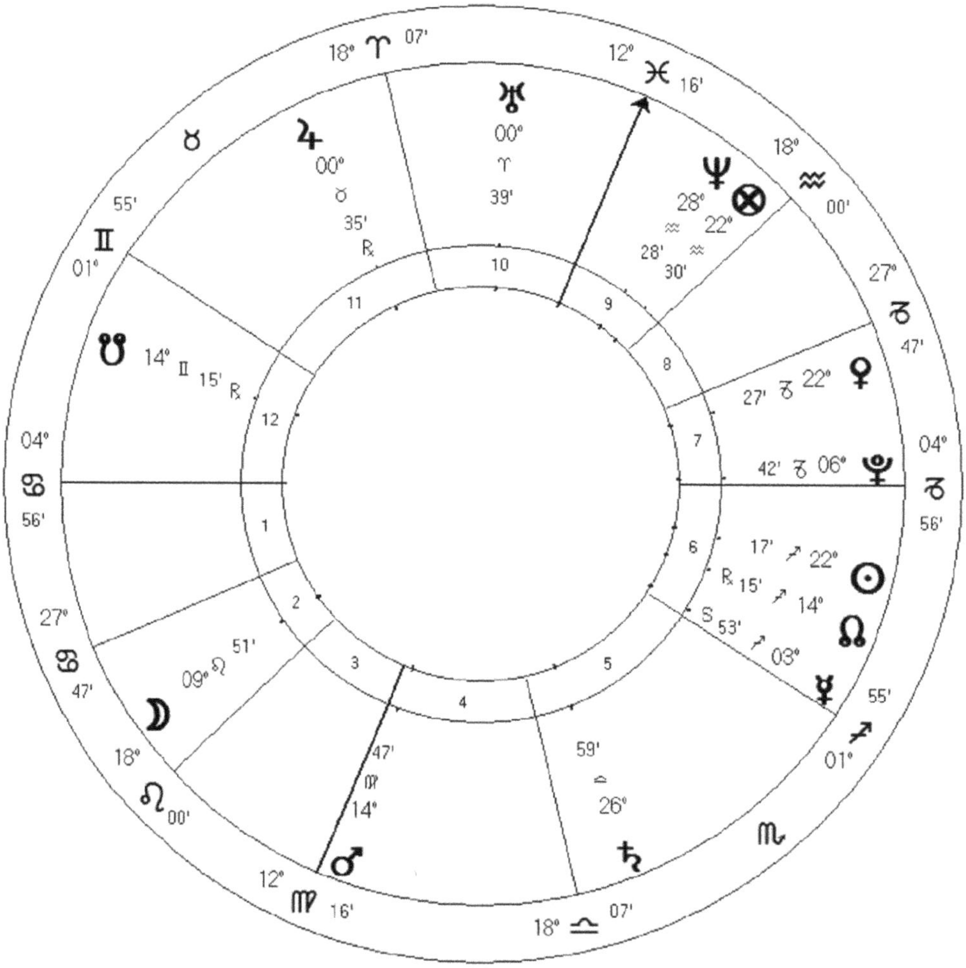

December 14, 2011, 5:51 P.M. | Thessaloniki, Greece | 4 Cancer

The querent is a woman who had chosen to stay single for some years after the painful end of a long-term relationship had left her heartbroken. She was now feeling ready to move on and enter a new relationship.

The question as she asked it is a good example of natural common sense: we must first find if there is the possibility for a relationship before we can give an answer to the "when" of that relationship.

The querent is represented by the Moon, which rules the 1st house in this chart, and also by Venus, because she is a woman. The quesited – the future boyfriend – is signified by the 7th house and its Lord Saturn, and also by the Sun, representing him in his role as a man.

Lord 1, the Moon, is located in Leo, the sign of the Sun: she is very interested – and also determined (fixed sign) to find a Man. She is also in the detriment of Saturn, which rules the 7th house: she doesn't know who the future mate will be, nor does she have anyone particular in mind. In the context of this question, this would mean that while she longs to find a man, she cannot find a specific individual who fits the bill.

Her other significator, Venus, is located in Capricorn, the sign of Lord 7, Saturn, so she as a woman is very keen on forming a relationship.

What is important here is that both her significators show a strong interest in what she is asking about. That is important because if we don't want something we don't take steps to pursue it and make it happen.

The quesited in his role as Man – the Sun – doesn't show any interest in the matter. As an individual personality he is signified by Saturn, which is in Libra. So Saturn is ruled by Venus (he wants to find a woman) and consequently we have a strong, positive, mutual reception (Venus in Saturn's sign; Saturn in Venus' sign) between him and her.

We have examined the various feelings and found that there is the possibility of a new relationship. Next is to find an aspect that will join the two people together, showing the relationship actually happening, and then to determine the timing at which this will take place.

There is a clear and immediate aspect – all the more encouraging because that aspect happens between Venus and Saturn, which are the two significators with this strong mutual reception. Venus will soon square Saturn. The aspect will perfect at 27:19 Libra, so Venus has to travel a little under 5 degrees to reach it. There is another aspect, as the Moon applies to trine the Sun, but the strong mutual reception between Venus and Saturn urges that judgement is based on that.

The timing: Venus is in a cardinal sign (fast) in an angular house (slow) which gives us the choice of the middle time-unit. The longest time-unit in such questions must be years, so the middle time would be a bit less than 5 months. And so it proved: she met him after 4 and half months.

Pregnancy & Children

Will I Conceive?

Molly Morrissey

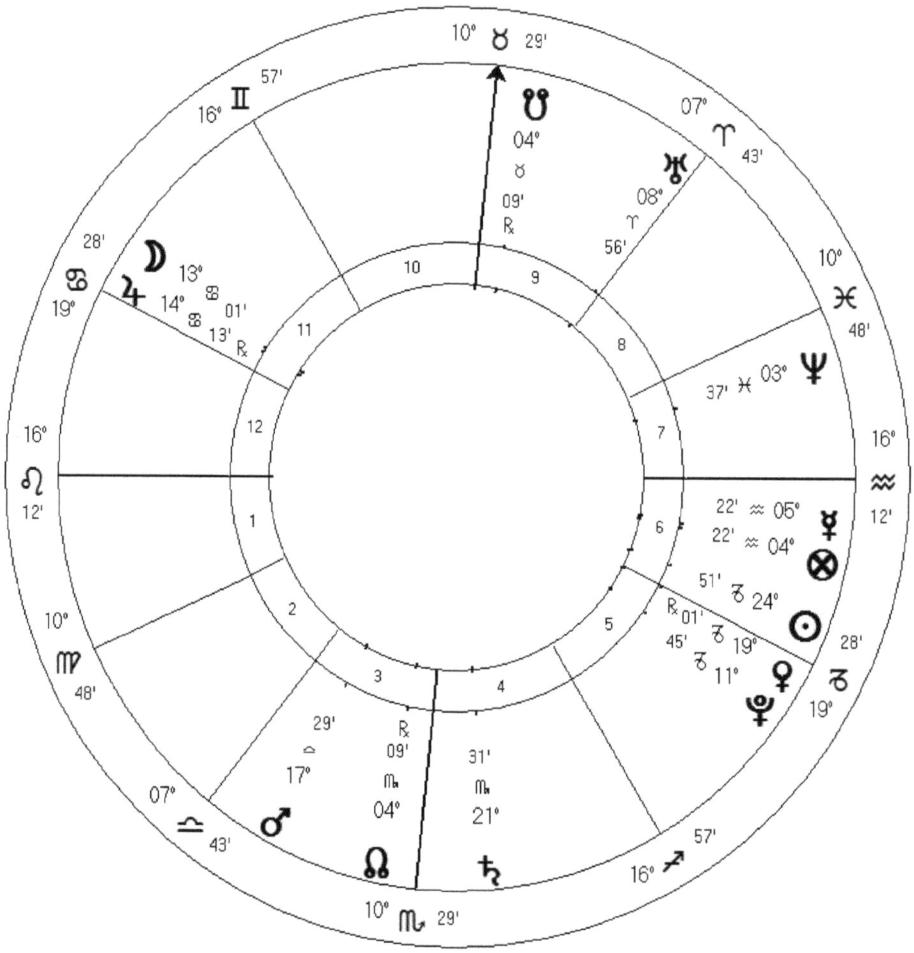

January 14, 2014, 6:43 P.M. | San Diego, CA | 16 Leo

The querent is an early 30s female, who had some medical issues and was worried she wouldn't be able to conceive a child. She and her husband had been trying to conceive for a while, with no positive result. She had not started infertility treatment but was working to support her health and knew she would consider treatment if it became necessary.

The querent gets Lord 1, the Sun, and the Moon. The baby gets Lord 5, Jupiter.
Because this woman is relatively young, the default answer is yes. I would keep an eye out for afflictions to the 1st house, the 5th and the 7th (representing her husband) anyhow, so no extra emphasis there even though she is concerned about medical issues.

The Moon is immediately applying to conjunct Lord 5. This is a major testimony for a yes to conception. This testimony is further strengthened by the Moon being very strong in its own sign and Jupiter being also strong in its exaltation. With both planets in the fertile sign of Cancer, the chart gives an absolute answer of yes, the querent will conceive.

In addition, there are no major afflictions to any of the houses in question. Jupiter is retrograde, which is a minor negative testimony, overruled by the abundance of positive ones. With Lord 1 tucked away in the 6th house, the querent is certainly interested in her own illness, though this interest isn't going to stop her from getting pregnant. That interest produced the anxiety that was driving the question.

Finally, the Moon is immediately applying to the conjunction with Jupiter. The conception will happen soon enough.

And so it proved. The querent reported being pregnant by the autumn of that same year.

When Will The Baby Come?

Molly Morrissey

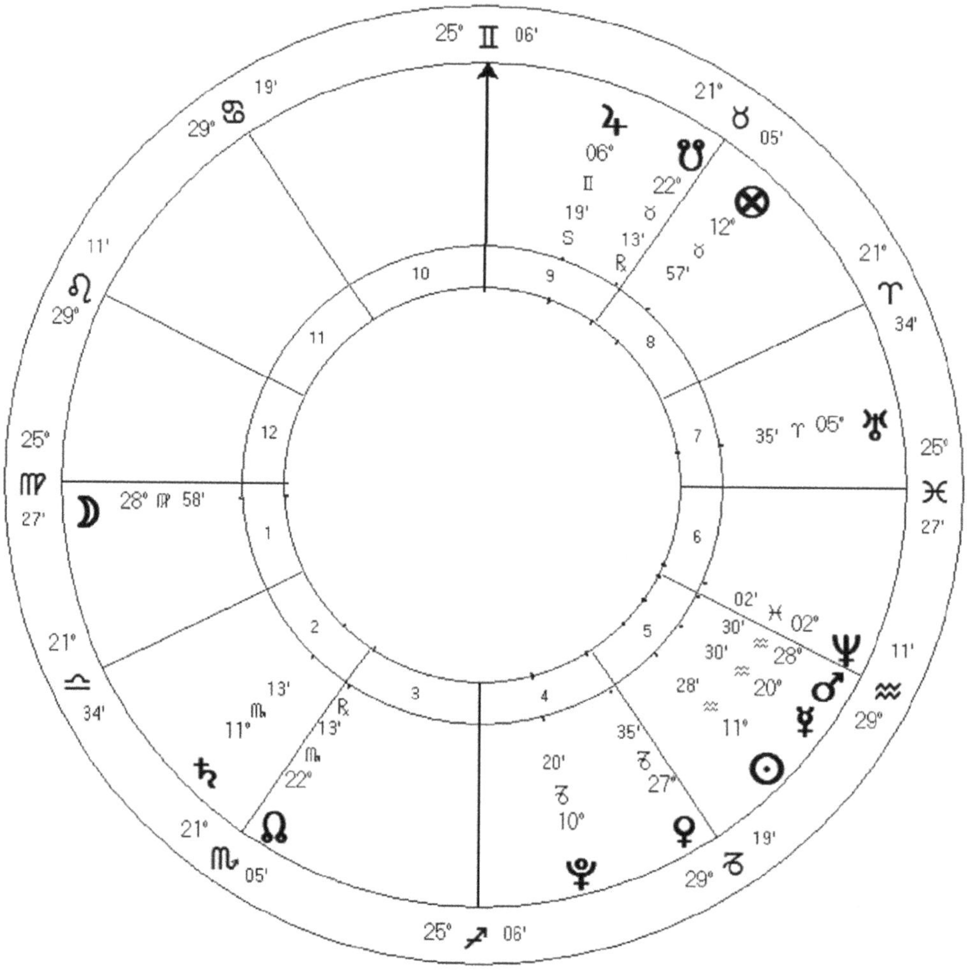

January 30, 2013, 8:45 P.M. | San Diego, CA | 25 Virgo

The querent was pregnant with her second child and due 6 weeks from the time the question was posed. Her midwife had given her a due date of March 10th and her doctor had given her a date of March 13th. Both mother and baby were healthy to the best of their knowledge, so this was not a motivation for the question. Mother had been having a variety of dreams and other intuitive indications that the baby would come early and was eager to see what the chart might show. Since the pregnancy was almost finished and couldn't go too far overdue or else she would be induced, we were looking for timing that showed anywhere from immediately to about 8 weeks out from the time of the question.

This chart was done before the *The Horary Textbook, Revised Edition* was published. In the original edition, timing a birth was not addressed, so I was on my own for the type of testimonies I was seeking. After giving it some thought, and speaking with a colleague, we came up with a variety of ideas.

We knew we weren't looking for an aspect between Lord 1 (the querent and mother) and Lord 5 (the baby) since they are already in closer contact than they ever will be again. We thought possible testimonies could be Lord 5 moving from a mutable sign into a cardinal sign or some change occurring within the first house, since it represents the body of the mother, though of course whatever that might be would need to make sense in the context of a birth. The third idea was to consider the Moon, as natural ruler of babies, changing sign.

Knowing that we ultimately are open to the way this particular chart wants to show the answer, we will always hold lightly our ideas of how the answer might be reflected, though holding tightly to a logical presentation of testimonies.

Looking at the chart, I was immediately struck by two testimonies. First, the Moon, natural ruler of babies, sits just inside the first house: a most elegant picture of baby inside mother. What is the Moon doing? Moving from final degrees of Virgo, a mutable sign, to Libra, a cardinal sign. This seems so far to be a strong representation of birth.

Can we get appropriate timing from this placement? With the Moon sitting at 28:58 of Virgo, it has just a bit over one degree to travel before the sign change. This would translate to just over a month away, which would be in range for the birth.

Looking around for other possible testimonies, I checked on both Lord 1 and Lord 5. Lord 1 is Mercury in the middle degrees of Aquarius, not doing anything that could remotely reflect a birth. Same goes for Lord 5, Saturn, sitting in the middle degrees of Scorpio. The best we can say here with Lord 1 in Aquarius, ruled by Lord 5, is that the mother is ruled by the child, which was true, as with the late days of any pregnancy where the mother's activity becomes very limited due to being so heavy with child. However, none of these testimonies give any possible timing indication.

The Moon in the first house about to move into a cardinal sign being the only reasonable testimony, it was used for the judgment. The Moon travels a small bit over one degree, so the timing would be just a day or two over one month away. I told the querent to expect delivery on March 1st, possibly the 2nd. Also, I didn't add more days just because February is a short month. A month is a month.

The querent gave birth midday on March 1st to a healthy child. In *The Horary Textbook, Revised Edition* Frawley has addressed this sort of chart and confirms that indeed, a planet changing signs will often give birth timing.

Will They Put the Baby Up for Adoption?

Kathryn Silvestre

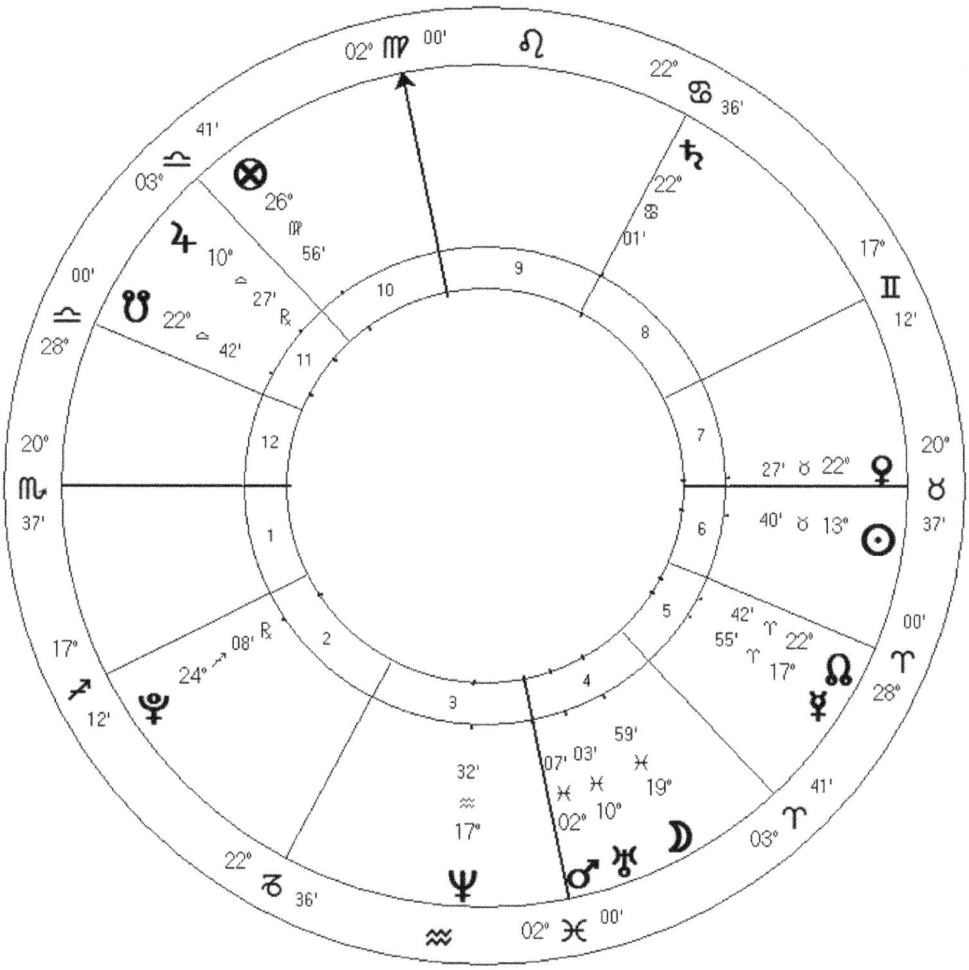

May 03, 2005, 8:09 P.M. | Selma, IN | 20 Scorpio

The querent knew of a young, unmarried couple who'd had a baby and were deciding whether to raise the baby themselves or put him up for adoption. The querent was a relative of one of the parents. She and her husband were very interested in adopting the child if the couple decided not to raise him themselves.

This chart is one of those that gives the answer with beauty and simplicity. The querent is Lord 1; the sign on the Ascendant is Scorpio, making Mars the querent's significator. The question is about someone else's child. "Someone else" is the seventh house; their child is the fifth from the seventh, which is the eleventh. The sign on cusp 11 is Libra, making Venus the significator of the child.

Look where Venus is: sitting just inside the seventh house, at home in its own, fixed sign of Taurus. The young couple will keep the baby. And so they did.

Am I Pregnant?

John Frawley

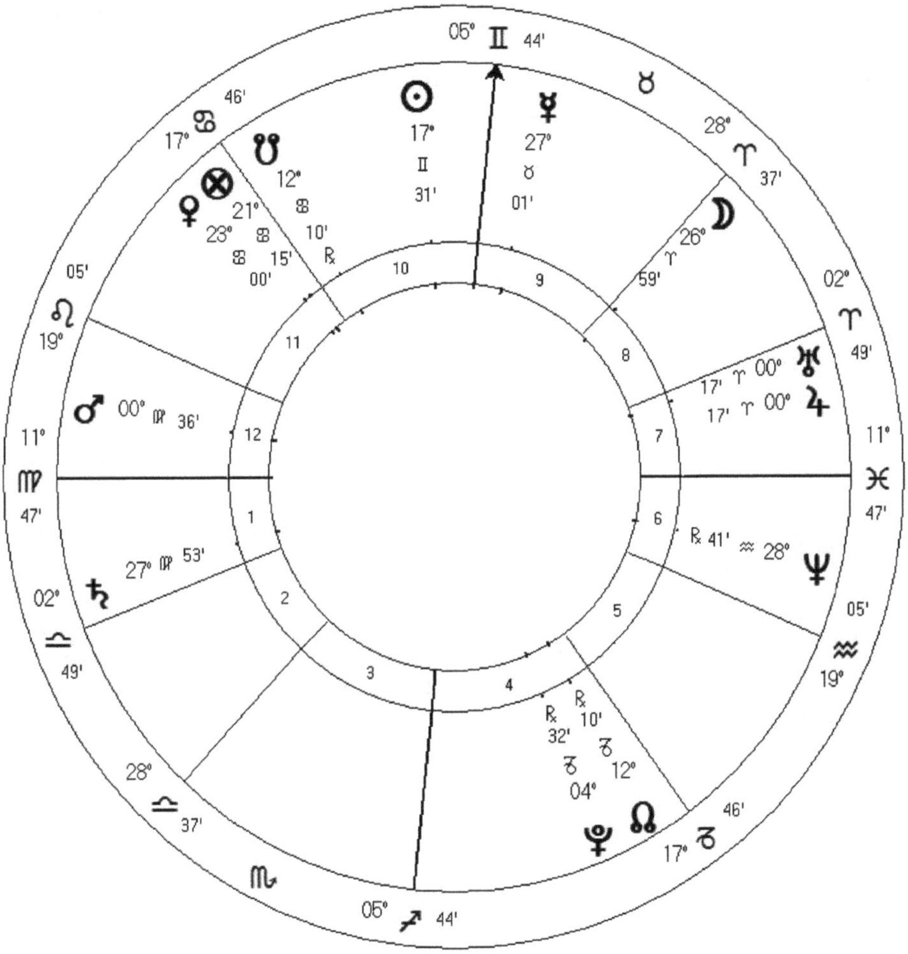

June 08, 2010, 12:01 P.M. | Poznan, Poland | 11 Virgo

With the ready availability of over-the-counter pregnancy testing, such questions are asked more often about the querent's cat or dog than about the querent herself. But as this chart shows, they do arise. The querent was hoping for a Yes.

The querent is signified by Mercury, ruler of the 1st house. The baby is shown by Lord 5, which is Saturn. We can use the Moon as cosignificator of the querent, but it is very much a secondary player in charts on this subject. Bring it in to judgement only if it thrusts itself forward, demanding our attention.

Saturn is in the 1st house. This can show the baby being inside Mum, which would give us the Yes that our querent is hoping for, but other testimonies, if such there are, must be considered too. Saturn is in Virgo, which is a barren sign, but that would be significant only in a general question about fertility or "Will I ever have a baby?" With the specific "Am I pregnant right now?" it can be ignored.

Saturn is also close to station. Lord 5 exactly in station would argue strongly against pregnancy: a planet in station is not moving, so does not support the idea of there being new life. This does *not* mean that a planet entering station is, in questions on any subject, testimony that the person that planet signifies will die. That I stop moving does *not* mean I'm dead: I could be dozing or watching TV. Saturn is moving at only 1 minute of arc per day, which is extremely slow, but compared to Saturn's usual lethargic motion it is still quite sprightly.

So far, so good. But there is another testimony: the aspect between Mercury (Mum) and Saturn (Baby). This aspect would connect Mum to Baby. Were it a separating aspect it would be a strong Yes: it would take some very powerful negatives to outweigh it. Here, the aspect is applying: it has not yet happened. If Mum is pregnant she is already as closely connected with Baby as is possible for her to be. So this aspect showing them becoming connected in the future is a definite No to the question about her being pregnant now.

This does not mean that the judgement here is, "You're not pregnant, but you soon will be". The question is about the querent's situation right now, and only that. "Soon" has no part of it. It is a still photograph, not a movie. Judgement is simply, "No, you're not"; which is as it proved to be.

When Will My Friend Have Her Baby?

Molly Morrissey

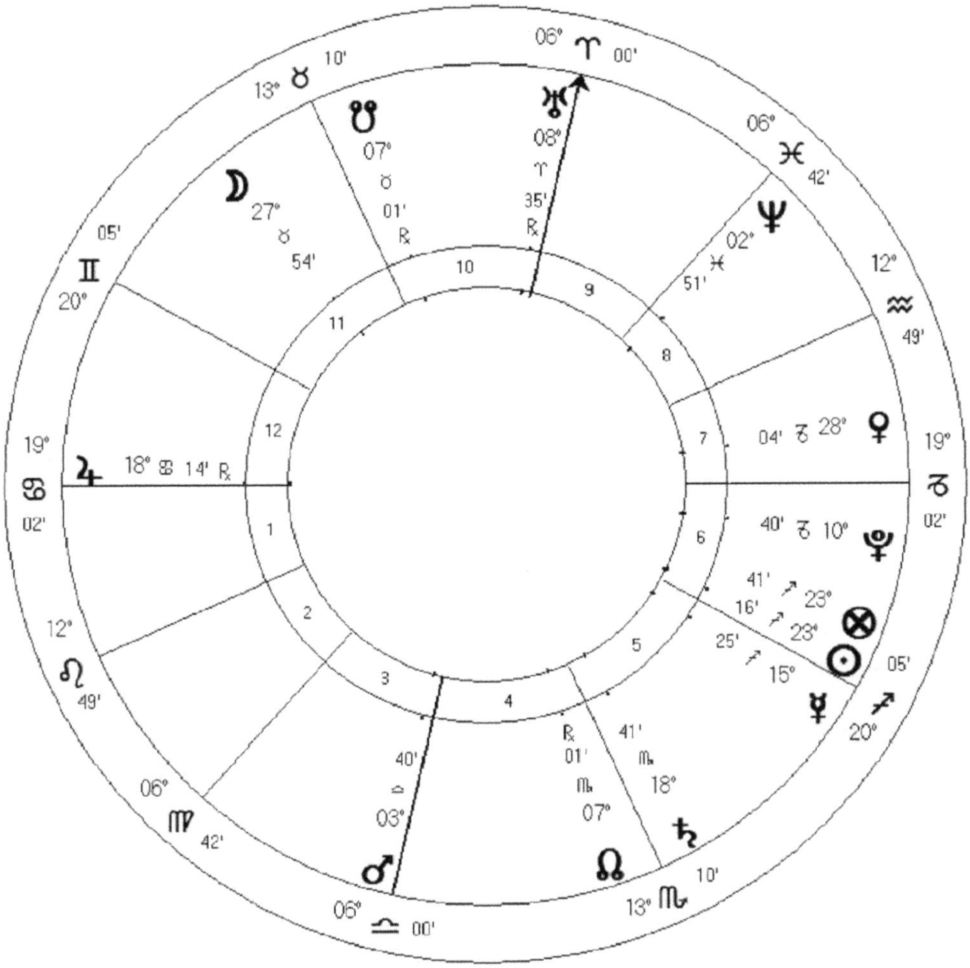

December 14, 2013, 6:35 P.M. | San Diego, CA | 19 Cancer

The querent had been chatting with her best friend, who was part way though a pregnancy. The expectant mother was considering buying a plane ticket for her mother to fly out and be present for the birth. The querent had called to ask if the chart could be done, and so it was. Later, the expectant mom emailed me and asked herself, directly, but ultimately, this initial chart held the correct answer. This is another example of where muddying the waters with multiple charts is the foolish choice. Mother was due on April 9th, so just under 4 months or 16.5 weeks from the date of the chart. Mother and baby were reported as healthy.

The querent is represented by Lord 1, the Moon. She's not the one having the baby, though, so her signifier is irrelevant. The mother-to-be is a very close friend of hers, and so in this case we can give the friend Lord 11, Venus. The baby would be 5th from the 11th, Lord 3, Mercury.

The strongest testimony would be a planet changing signs, maybe a planet in the mother's house doing something interesting. I was not looking for an aspect.

Venus is going to change sign in two degrees, into a fixed sign. The 2 degrees it travels to the sign cusp doesn't correspond much with our time frame. It could indicate a premature birth, but the change of sign into fixed doesn't make sense. The Moon, natural ruler of babies, is also not in the right time frame with three degrees to travel. But again, this planet could give testimony for an early birth.

Lord 5, Mercury, the baby's signifier, is in a mutable sign travelling into cardinal. Mercury needs to travel fourteen and a half degrees to get to the cardinal sign. This put the baby's birth into the right time frame.

The 14 + degrees put the birth at the week starting the 22nd of March. Because of the half degree, I'd given a mid-week date of March 24-27th as the birth date.

I got the date wrong by a day. The baby was born on March 23rd. Both mother and baby were healthy. The lesson here is that if the unit is weeks, stick with that and don't split hairs.

Is There Anything Wrong With the Baby? When It Will Be Born?

Marcos Monteiro

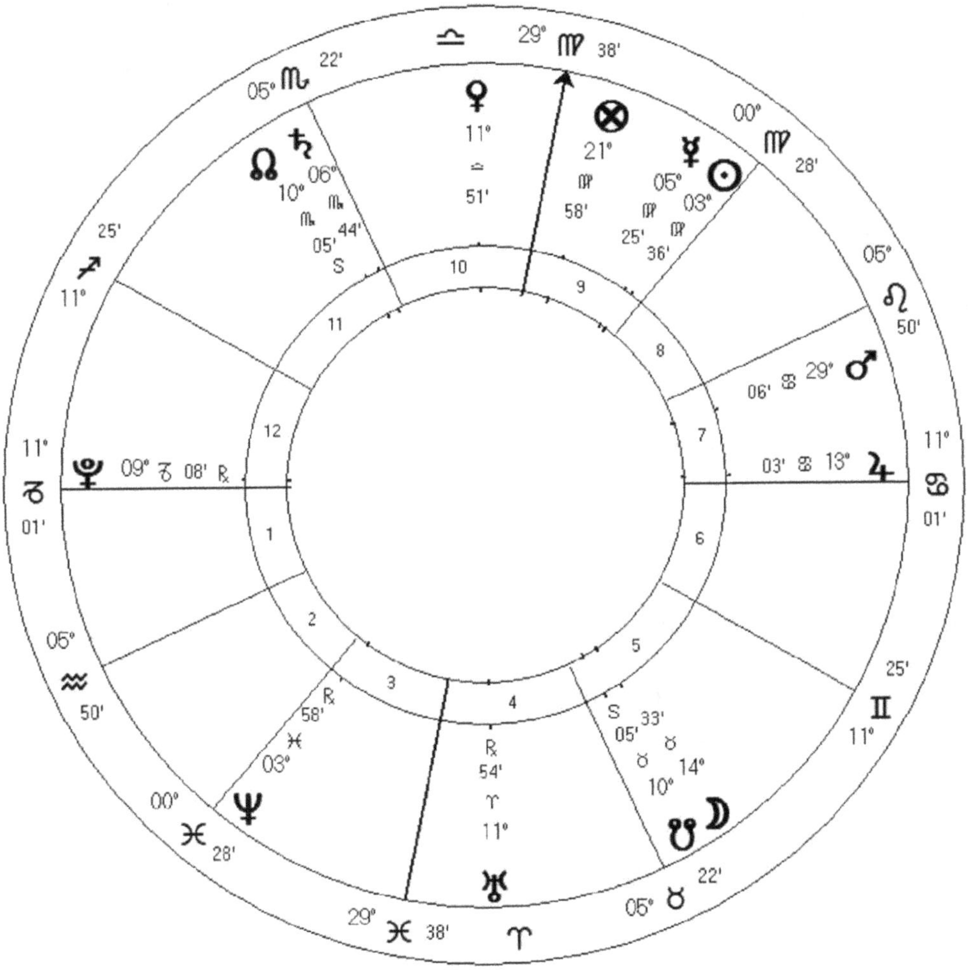

August 26, 2013, 1:53 P.M. | Barra Velha/SC, Brazil | 11 Capricorn

The querent was pregnant and, in theory, about to deliver. However, she felt no contractions. Although there were no previous health issues either with her or the baby, she was worried that something might be wrong, and wanted to know when the birth would happen.

The querent is Saturn, ruler of Capricorn on the first cusp. Saturn is not in particularly good condition, but it's not afflicted in any way: it's in a neutral house, in neither its detriment nor its fall. It is closely aspected by a very dignified Mercury, which means no harm to it (Mercury is not in any of Saturn's debilities): nice. It is heading towards the expansive North Node, which is descriptive: she's about to birth a baby. So far, so good.

Is the child in any danger? The child is signified by Venus, ruler of the fifth house of children (inside or outside the womb). Venus is in Libra, its own sign and in the exaltation and triplicity of Saturn: the child seems fine and, moreover, doesn't pose any problem to the mother.

What will happen to them? Saturn will sextile Mercury. Venus will square Jupiter. Oh, no! Jupiter is the lord of the 12th house of self-undoing, anguish and all those terrible things all astrological authors warn us against; it's the worst house in the sky. Jupiter is in Saturn's detriment, opposing the querent's cusp. On top of that, it's the 8th house from the 5th, it's the house of the death of the baby!

No, not really. These things must be seen in the context of the question. The pregnancy had been normal up to that point: the mother was healthy, and as far as she could tell the baby was fine, and the chart supports that. Venus in Libra is doing quite well, and Saturn in Scorpio is not particularly afflicted. Jupiter must be something else.

The 12th house is also the house of childbed. Jupiter is just inside the seventh house, at the hands of the ruler of that house, as it were. The seventh could mean the querent's husband, but it also means someone important in this context: the doctor, the partner of the querent in this situation.

Why is Jupiter at the hands of the doctor? Well, one possible explanation is that the baby would be born via C-section. This is congruent with the imminent aspect between Saturn and Mercury (the ruler of the sixth house of surgeries). The querent had mentioned that this was a possibility.

When will the birth happen? Both relevant aspects point to one unit of time. There isn't really much option here: "days" is the only unit that fits the bill.

My judgment was that the baby was OK, and that the querent would deliver soon, in one or two days.

The querent started to feel contractions the day after she asked the question, doctors decided to perform a C-section, the baby – a boy – was born perfectly healthy, and the mother was fine.

Any Chance of Having My Own Child?

Kathryn Silvestre

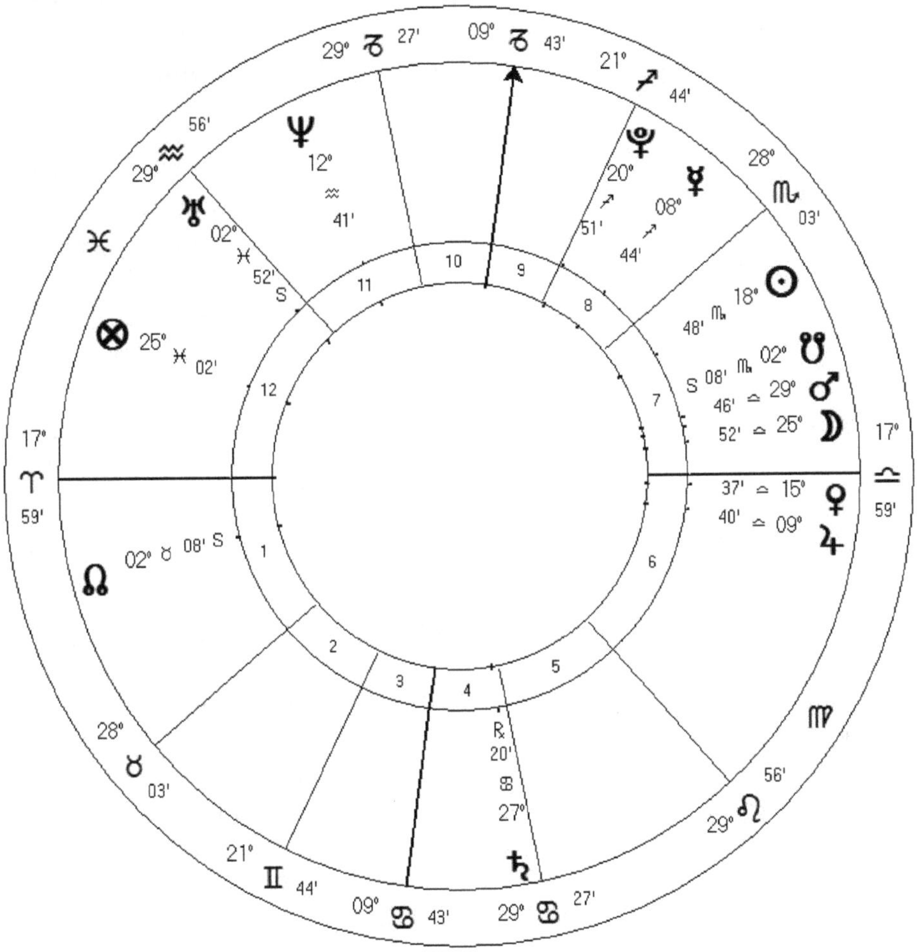

November 10, 2004, 4:02 P.M. | Selma, IN | 17 Aries

The querent was in her mid-forties, recently married and trying to conceive a child. Neither she nor her spouse had any children previously. The fertility specialist had told her she was unlikely to get pregnant without a donor egg. The querent very much wanted her own biological child, and so came to consultation wanting to know if this was possible. Secondarily, she wanted to know if she could have a successful pregnancy with a donor egg.

Aries rises, so our querent is Mars, ruler of Aries. Normally we would also give the querent the Moon as cosignificator, but with Cancer on the fifth house cusp, the Moon must play the more important role of her potential child.

This question has two parts. First, we look for testimonies for or against the querent's having her own child. For this we need a plausible way to bring Lord 1, Mars, and Lord 5, the Moon, together by conjunction or aspect.

The Moon, at 25:52 of Libra, applies to conjunct Mars at 29:46 Libra. But before the Moon can conjunct Mars it perfects a square with Saturn at 27:20 Cancer. Does this square prohibit the conjunction with Mars that follows? To find out we must look at both dignity and, especially, reception. The Moon is not happy where it is in Libra (in the via combusta), though it is accidentally strong in the angular 7th house. But reception is key here. The Moon in Libra exalts Saturn; Saturn in Cancer loves the Moon. This is strong mutual reception. By virtue of placement in Libra the Moon also hates Mars. Taken together, these testimonies tell us that the Moon's square to Saturn does, in fact, prohibit the conjunction with Mars that comes after.

Unfortunately for our querent, this is clear testimony for judging. No to part one of her question, whether she will have her own biological child.

The second part of the question asks if she will have a successful pregnancy via donor egg. This time Saturn has a different role to play as Lord 11, the fifth house from the seventh. This is the child-potential of someone else; in other words, the donor egg. The Moon in this scenario brings Saturn and Mars together by translation of light. The Moon makes contact first with Saturn by square and then carries Saturn's light with it to Mars. This shows the possibility of conception.

We must now look at receptions to see if the conception is supported. Alas, the difficult reception between Mars and Saturn raises concerns. Mars exalts Saturn – showing the querent's strong interest in a child – but Saturn takes Mars into fall. Not only that, but the Moon, as carrier, further antagonizes Mars by taking Mars into detriment. Mars is vulnerable to begin with in Libra, but then gets this one-two punch from Saturn and the Moon. At best these receptions show difficulties in the process of in vitro fertilization; at worst they suggest that a pregnancy might not be viable.

The couple continued with fertility treatments but, in the end, stopped short of attempting in vitro fertilization, either with her own or a donor egg. The querent's dream of having a child was never realized.

Health

Where's the Inflammation?

Fotini Christodoulou

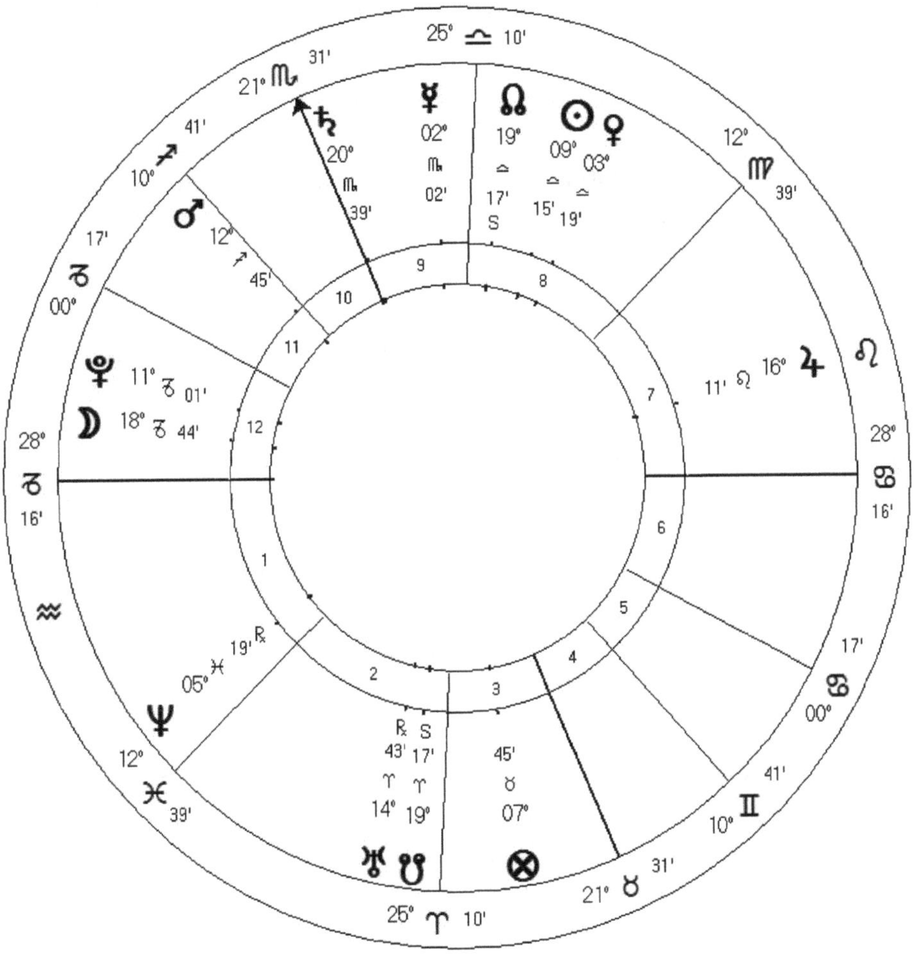

October 02, 2014, 4:00 P.M. | Thessaloniki, Greece | 28 Capricorn

The querent had different health issues, but he was at the moment interested in finding the location of a particular inflammation that was causing him a general loss of vitality. This inflammation was shown in medical tests but the doctors could not locate the part of the body where it lay. So, the querent was having random tests in case he was able to discover the problem by chance.

The querent is signified by Lord 1, Saturn: a cold dry planet in a cold moist sign, afflicted then by its dispositor, Mars, which we find at 12:45 Sagittarius in the 11th house of the chart. Richard Saunders (see Glossary) writes about this placement: "Mars is hot and dry above nature, consuming and drying up the radical moisture and humidity of the body and utterly extinguishing the life of man;" matching what the querent has told us about his loss of vitality.

As always in medical questions each house points to a part of the body, starting with the first house which represents the head. Finding Mars in the 11th house, we should theoretically look for the inflammation somewhere below the knees. But the querent indicated that this part of the body had no signs of something pointing to an inflammation. However the chart has the answer somewhere: it demands to be looked at differently.

We find the Moon separating from an antiscion contact to Mars and applying to sextile Lord 1, Saturn: a symptom that has not yet appeared and is connected with both Mars and Lord 1. The Moon is also in square to the Nodal axis, as if the chart wishes to draw the attention to it. Saunders writes, among other things, that this placement of the Moon is connected with strangury (painful urination). The Moon rules the 7th house of the chart representing the reproductive system, which not only can fit Saunders' suggestion, but more importantly agrees with Mars, our primary suspect, which is naturally associated with the gall bladder and male genitals. All players suggest that the problem lies somewhere in the reproductive system.

The querent didn't have such problems at the time of the consultation, but the relevant test results he received the next day, showed a serious inflammation of the prostate, confirming the judgment: and as the applying aspect showed (the Moon sextile Saturn) the new symptom of strangury appeared the day after the consultation.

Am I Overworking?

John Frawley

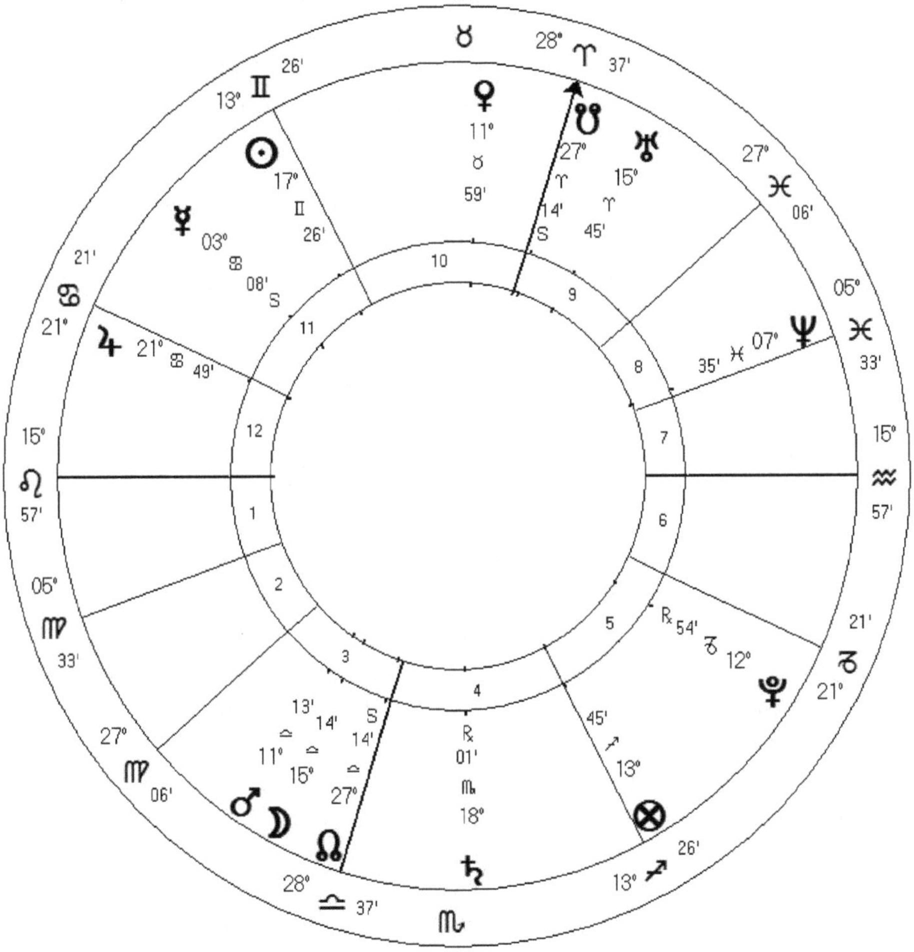

June 08, 2014, 9:16 A.M. | Warsaw, Poland | 15 Leo

The client had a demanding and stressful full-time job. On top of this, she had for a long time been working all weekend to help with a family business, work that she found physically exhausting. She asked, “Can I keep up with this weekend work for another year or two, or do I have to calm down, so I don’t hit a burn-out?” Other than some slight editing for anonymity, I have presented this judgement as it was given to the client. She had previously asked another question about some problems in the day-job.

This chart could hardly be clearer: yes, you do need to calm down! You cannot continue like this without there being a price to pay.

The South Node is right on the cusp – the point of emphasis – of the 10th house, the house of work. This is a strong testimony of problems from work. These problems will be those relevant to the context of this question, so this is not a restatement of the issues we discussed in the previous judgement.

The ruler of the 10th house, hence significator of your work situation, is Mars. Mars is in the "fall" of the Sun, which, as Lord 1, signifies you. This is quite literal: it brings you down. This is exacerbated by the Moon, also in the fall of the Sun, which "translates the light" of Mars to the Sun, i.e. it brings home this malign effect, making it real rather than potential.

Your planet, the Sun, is on the fixed star Rigel, which is in the foot of Orion. Fixed stars are rarely relevant in horary, but this one has a clear and specific relevance to the situation asked about. Orion thought he was big and strong and tough, and could defeat anything. But no: Diana, the Moon-goddess (change over time) sent the scorpion (symbolic of the natural limitations of our existence as human beings), which defeated him. The foot of any creature is seen as the consequence of that creature's nature (because it leaves footprints), so this is the unfortunate but inevitable consequence of Orion thinking he was so big and strong and tough. This is a strong and clear testimony that there will be a price to pay if you carry on working like this.

Or, to put it another way, try being a bit nice to yourself!

I hope this is helpful. As before, I will remind you that I am not infallible.

Not long after the client wrote to say that she had carried on with the weekend job as before, but had now had to stop after suffering a stress fracture – in her foot.

What's the Problem With My Stomach? What Can I Do to Relieve It?

Marcos Monteiro

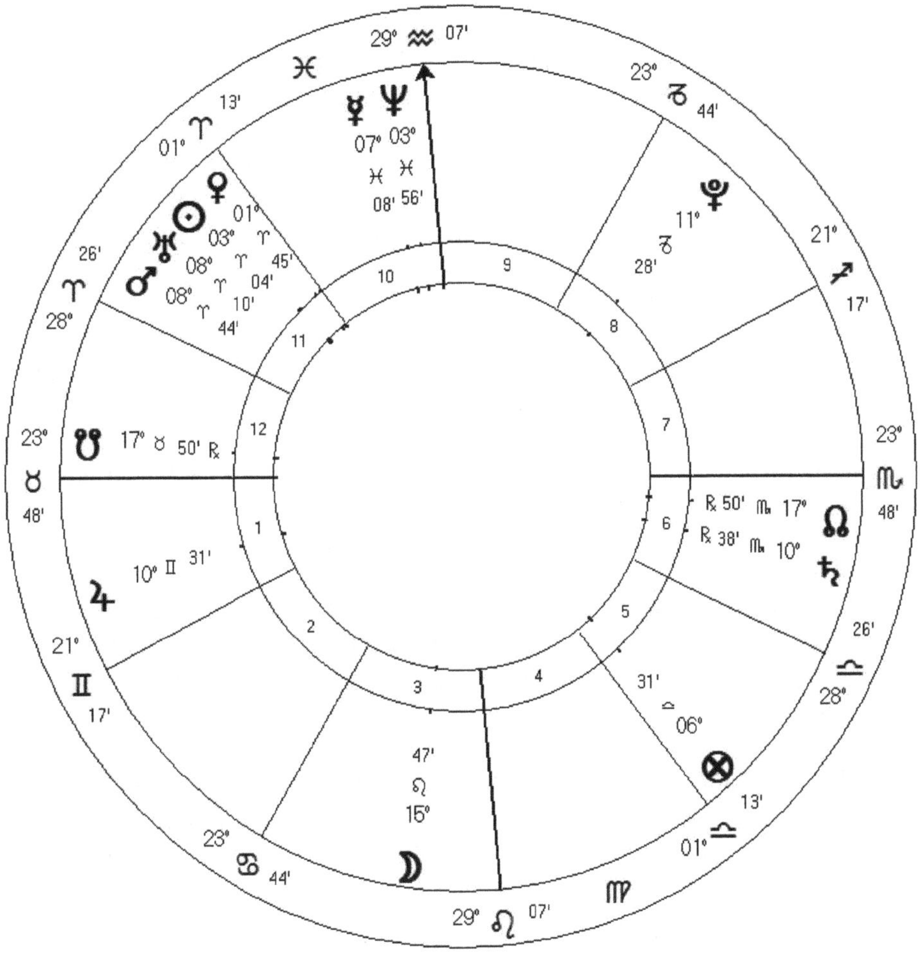

March 23, 2013, 10:15 A.M. | Barra Velha/SC, Brazil | 23 Taurus

I felt a huge pain in my stomach. I wanted to know what was going on and, more importantly, what I could do to relieve it.

I am Venus, ruler of Taurus on the first cusp. My stomach is the ruler of the sign on the 5th cusp: it's also Venus, the ruler of Libra.

This is not a problem. I don't need to compare the rulers, or analyze an aspect between me and my stomach.

Venus is in Aries, in its detriment: a bad state. More than that, it is in a hot and dry sign and combust: burned by the hot and dry Sun. Both testimonies point to an excess of the fiery humor choler. This conjunction is on the eleventh cusp – opposing the 5th cusp, emphasizing that this was the problem.

Planets in the detriment of Venus harm it. Besides Venus itself and the Sun, there is another planet in Venus's detriment– the fiery planet, Mars.

So, I have a big excess of heat and dryness in the stomach. To alleviate the problem (and help it go away), I need cold and moisture: water, cold and moist food, fruit juice, etc. I also had to cut out hot and dry food (pepper, garlic, onion, coffee, etc.).

That is the problem. But what is at the root of it, its cause? It's no good to cure a local problem by worsening the overall imbalance; I had to check the underlying humoral excess.

To see that, I must look at Venus again, but now as me. It's a cold and moist planet in a hot and dry sign, so it is unbalanced. The ruler of the sign is probably the cause of this humoral disequilibrium.

This is Mars in Aries, again. The humor in excess is the nature of the sign, fire or choler. The symptoms tend to be related to the planet – in this case, Mars. No doubt about it, my problem was choler excess, which manifested in my stomach.

Cold and moist food and drinks improved my condition very much. I didn't follow the diet strictly, however (Magician, heal thyself!), and it came back again after a while. Then, I realized I really had to change my diet and start drinking more water. And so I did.

Will Dad Die Soon? If So, When?

Molly Morrissey

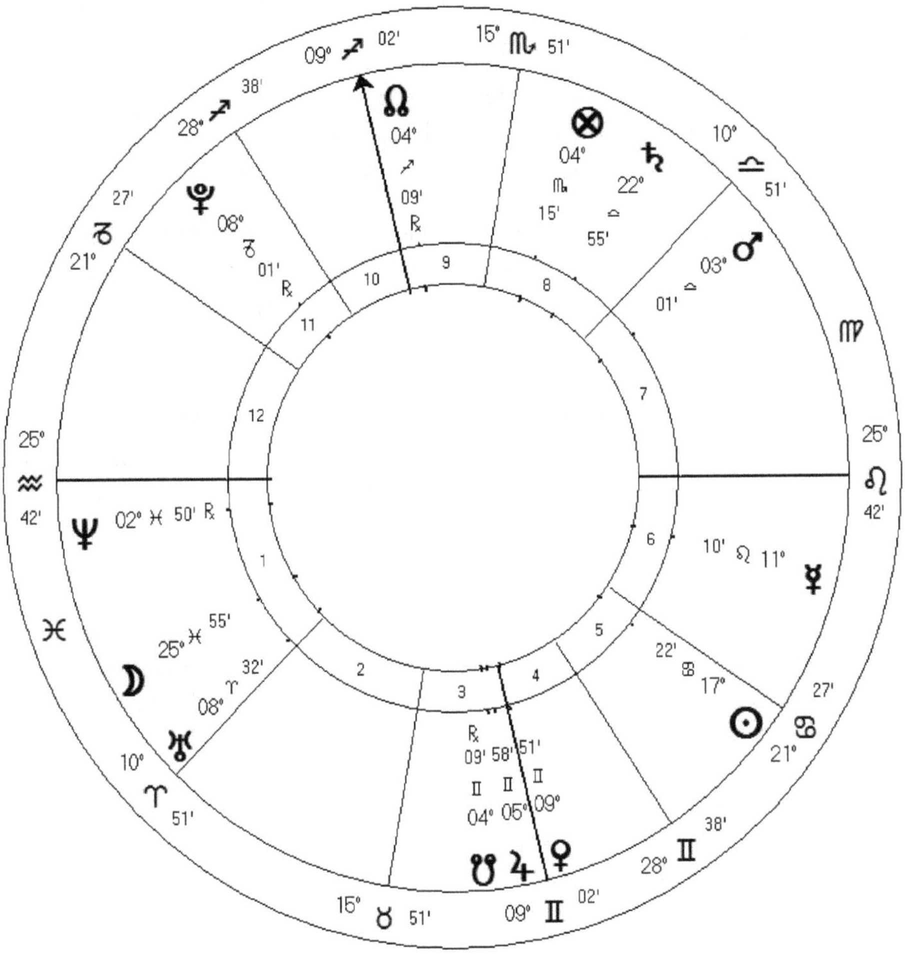

July 08, 2012, 10:25 P.M. | Placitas, NM | 25 Aquarius

For a variety of reasons, I was concerned about the possibility of my dad dying soon. Shortly after I asked the question and erected the chart, he announced he would be taking a road trip from Oregon, where he was living, to Kansas, where he'd grown up, at the end of September of that year. He was 85 years old at the time.

My dad gets Lord 4, Mercury. Death is signified by Lord 8. We would consider both radical Lord 8, Venus, and turned Lord 8 (Lord 11), Jupiter. Mercury is approaching a station to retrograde. Venus perfects a sextile with Mercury within minutes of arc before Mercury actually stations retrograde.

When I initially cast the chart, I wasn't sure what to make of this aspect and then station, so I set it aside.

A few days later when he announced intentions for his road trip, a drive he'd made many dozens of times in his life, I went back and looked a little closer. The aspect perfects at just under 3 degrees travel time for Venus.

In translating that to real time, the appropriate time units would be "weeks, months, or years" since I was considering if something would happen relatively soon. Since Mercury is moving very slowly as it comes to station, Venus is the faster moving planet and the one that I considered for judging the timing. Venus is angular and mutable. Angular would indicate the slowest and mutable would indicate the middle. Accordingly, I chose the middle time unit, which in this case was months. This gave me timing of a little less than 3 months from the time the question was asked, or the beginning of October.

I had also noticed that Venus is ruled by Mercury. Jupiter is, too, for that matter. I somehow managed to get both of the death signifiers on the cusp of the fourth house. The placements are interesting, but mean nothing in terms of judgment. If Mercury had been in a sign ruled by either Venus or Jupiter, the mutual reception would have been testimony for dad being spared. But alas, that is not the case here. There is no mutual reception with Mercury in Sun-ruled Leo.

The chart boils down to this question: Does the Mercury sextile with Venus prohibit the retrograde, or does the station show my father staying put, not going anywhere?

I was not sure and held it all very lightly, though with some concern as October approached. I was not convinced the aspect would win out, and of course emotionally did not want it to.
In reality, this is what happened:

My dad left on his trip with a bad cough. On Oct 1st he overshot the highway exit where his hotel was and kept driving another 2 hours north into Nebraska. He finally pulled over from delirium and a truck driver who noticed him collapsed in his car called the paramedics. He was taken to a small community hospital in a small town in Nebraska – where he received the highest level of care. They had him stabilized within a few days. It turned out that his bad cough was pneumonia, which continued to intensify as the trip progressed. The doctor (and the sheriff who was at the scene and took his car) were both very concerned that he could have died and remarked upon the various key moments where dad got lucky. Death was prohibited; my father stayed right where he was.

Ultimately, the chart showed Mercury's stationing retrograde as testimony that my dad wasn't going anywhere: a graceful and fascinating example of the literal translation horary is capable of producing.

Will Mum's Tumor Stop Growing?

Fotini Christodoulou

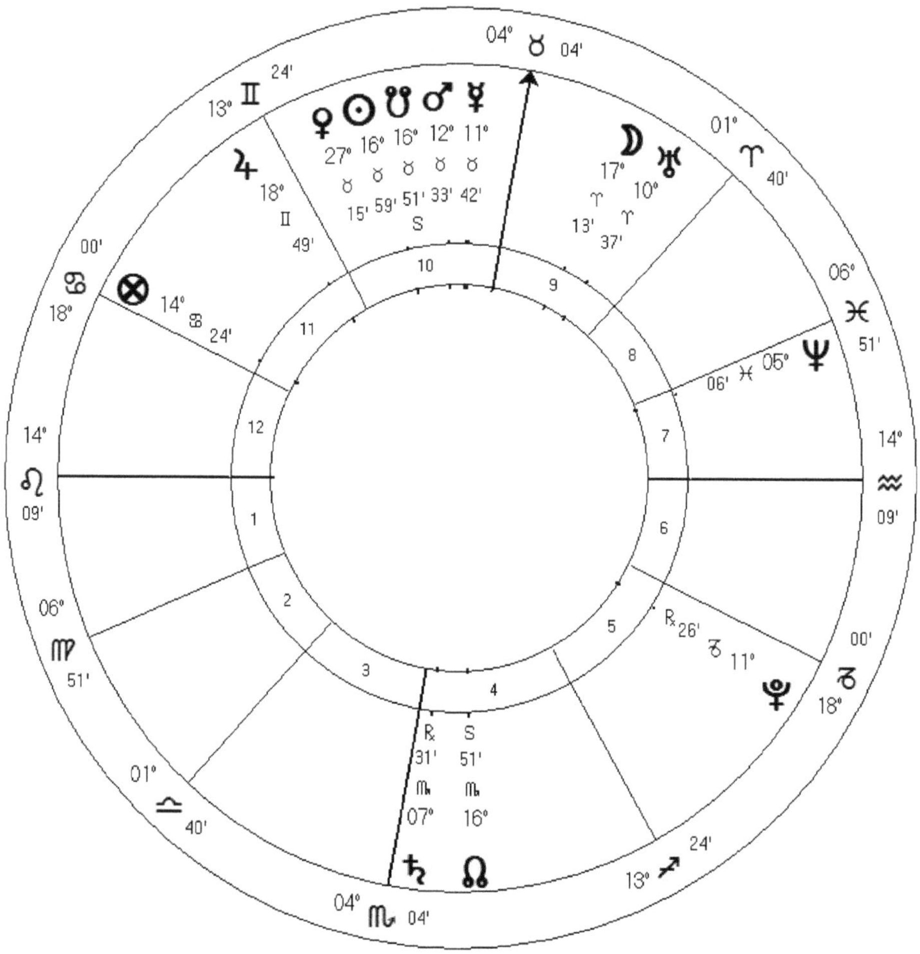

May 07, 2013, 12:34 P.M. | Thessaloniki, Greece | 14 Leo

The querent's mother was diagnosed with a meningioma, a benign kind of – slow growing – tumor in the head. This tumor was, however, causing short-term memory problems and it was also related with a mild case of depression, but it wasn't considered dangerous as long as it kept the same slow rate of development. The querent wanted to know whether it would stop growing or if, at the least, would keep its slow rhythm of development so that the problems it caused would be more or less stabilized.

The querent's mother is signified by the 10th house at 4:05 Taurus and its Lord Venus. As it is a medical question the cusp of the 10th house can be seen as the 1st house of the mother, so it represents her head, which is the part of the body that concerns us, consequently we look for afflictions to this cusp.

As always the chart will be tailored to the question: we find Saturn inside the radical 4th but as it is in retrograde motion and close to the 4th cusp, it can be seen as being on the cusp; therefore opposing/harming the 10th, which is representing mother's head. And it is a very appropriate significator for the tumor: Saturn, a slow moving planet, in a fixed sign. Saturn, as mentioned, is retrograde in motion and its speed is close to its average, which means that at the moment the tumor is growing to its usual slow rhythm. The question is if it will stop growing. Taking a look at the ephemeris we can see that Saturn will station at 4:49 degrees of Scorpio. So following the natural process of the body, the tumor gradually lowers its speed of growing and stabilizes. I should note that the chart doesn't of course suggest that the tumor will disappear; what we see must be judged against the context we have. It'll be in the same placement afflicting mother's head but at least, it will not get out of control. That's all we need to know to answer this question.

Later medical tests confirmed the judgment.

Will I Die Soon?

John Frawley

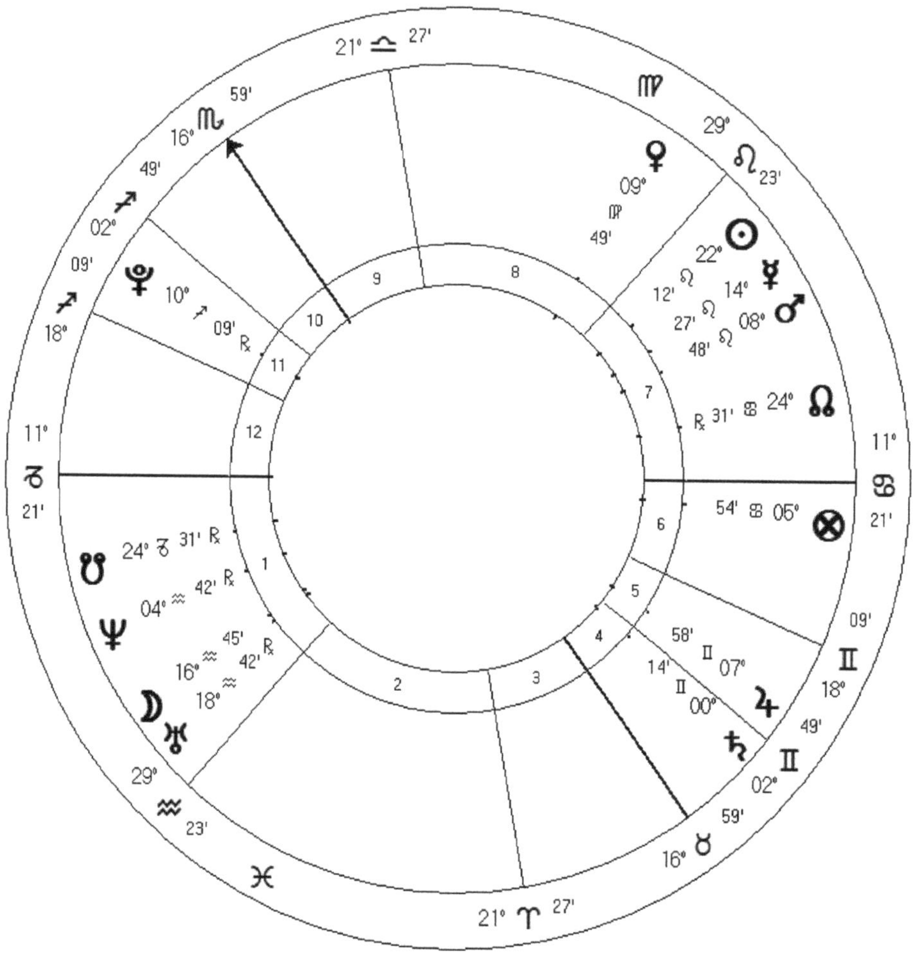

August 14, 2000, 6:25 P.M. | London, England | 11 Capricorn

The querent was an elderly man on a limited income. He didn't want to waste money paying the premiums on a life assurance policy if he would not die within its term. He asked, "Will I die within the next two years?"

The querent is signified by Saturn, ruler of the 1st house. That this is Saturn rather than any other planet is of no significance: our querent would be just as elderly whichever planet represented him. Don't use the Moon as the querent's cosignificator in a question like this. When death is certain and the question asks only about its timing, we can use the Moon as cosignificator of the querent. But doing that when, as here, the question is if death will happen, would have us predicting death far too readily.

Saturn's condition in the chart is of no interest to us. We are not concerned with our querent's health, but only in the Yes or No of whether he will die. His significator could be in the most parlous condition, yet he could live out these two years; it could be in robust condition, showing him glowing with health, yet he could die in an accident tomorrow.

Death is signified by the Lord of the 8th house, which is the Sun. The Sun will perfect a square aspect to Saturn. This would show the querent's death. But before that aspect perfects the Moon makes an opposition to the Sun. This prohibits the Sun/Saturn aspect, preventing it happening. So no, he will not die. If we were using the Moon as his cosignificator its aspect to the ruler of the 8th would be clear testimony that he would die, so the decision on whether or not we do so is an important one. If death were certain, as in the open-ended question "When will I die?", we would read this aspect as an event happening along the way, but in a question that is "if" not "when" it prohibits.

Even did it not, the Sun's aspect to Saturn would not give a Yes to the question. That aspect does not perfect until after the Sun has changed sign. If the question contains a time-limit, the end of the planets' present sign marks that limit. If the aspect doesn't perfect before that, the event will not happen within that time. This aspect will perfect immediately after the Sun changes sign, but this does not mean that the querent will die immediately after these two years end. The question asks only for a Yes or a No, so anything in the chart other than that is irrelevant. When the Sun reaches the end of its sign without having aspected Saturn, that is the end of the story. Nothing that it does thereafter matters.

The querent saved his money and saw out his two years.

Will Darryl Die?

Marcos Monteiro

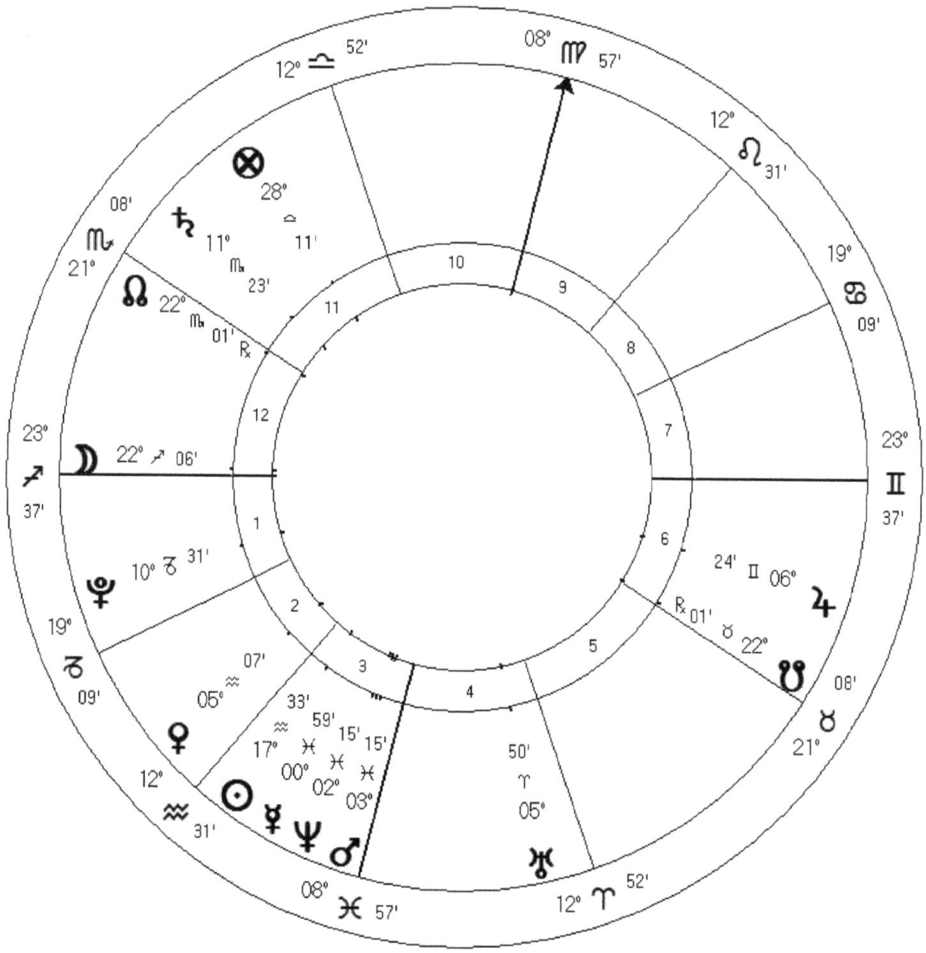

February 06, 2013, 2:51 A.M. | Barra Velha/SC, Brazil | 23 Sagittarius

I was a huge fan of the *Walking Dead* series, and Darryl Dixon was by far my favorite character. The producers made it very difficult for the audience to have favorite characters, however; lots of people got killed all the time. (I use the past tense because I don't watch it any longer.)

The season ended as if Darryl's time had come. He was captured, forced to fight against his own brother, Merle (at that time, working for the bad guy) who seemed quite OK with punching and stabbing the hell out of his little brother.

They were in an arena, full of the Governor's people. The Governor himself and his guards were there, fully armed and bloodthirsty. Oh, did I mention the zombies? They were surrounding the brothers, tied to chains; if any of the Dixons stepped too close, that was it.

I couldn't wait for the next season to start! I had to know if Darryl would make it out alive.

Darryl is not related to me in any way, he's "another person". So, he gets the 7th house, in Gemini, and its ruler, Mercury.

Mercury's in terrible state. It has just entered its detriment and fall. Mercury's conjunct Neptune and applies to a conjunction to Mars – which rules the 12th house of prison and captivity and, in Pisces, hates Mercury.

This is not good – but it doesn't mean he will die. People don't die of an accumulation of bad things. We can only die by death – astrologically, by some kind of contact with the ruler of the 8th house.

Since the question is not about the querent's death, we have to watch both rulers: the ruler of the radical eighth house, "death" (the Moon), and the ruler of the 2nd house, the turned 8th, "his death" (Saturn).

The Moon is just on the Ascendant, stressing that I'm thinking about death (it is weighing on me), but it does not aspect Mercury.

Mercury could aspect Saturn, but before it does, it will conjunct Mars, which prohibits the aspect.

Good. So far, Darryl lives. But there is another testimony.

Saturn is at 11:23 of Scorpio; its antiscion falls at 18:37 (and will move backwards as Saturn moves forward bodily). The Sun is at 17:34 of Aquarius and will conjunct Saturn's antiscion in about one degree. Antiscia can prohibit aspects, although it's less likely than bodily aspects. We don't need this prohibition, because we have the Mars-Mercury conjunction; but it tells us another thing. There is something interposing itself between Darryl and death – by antiscion, hidden somehow. This something is signified by the Sun in Aquarius, almost as bad off as Mercury is.

The Sun rules the 9th house, which is the turned 3rd, the house of Darryl's siblings. Could this mean that Merle would actually help his little brother? It seemed so: and in a hidden way, behind the Governor's back.

Darryl survived. Merle did try his best to help him.

Is It Multiple Sclerosis?

John Frawley

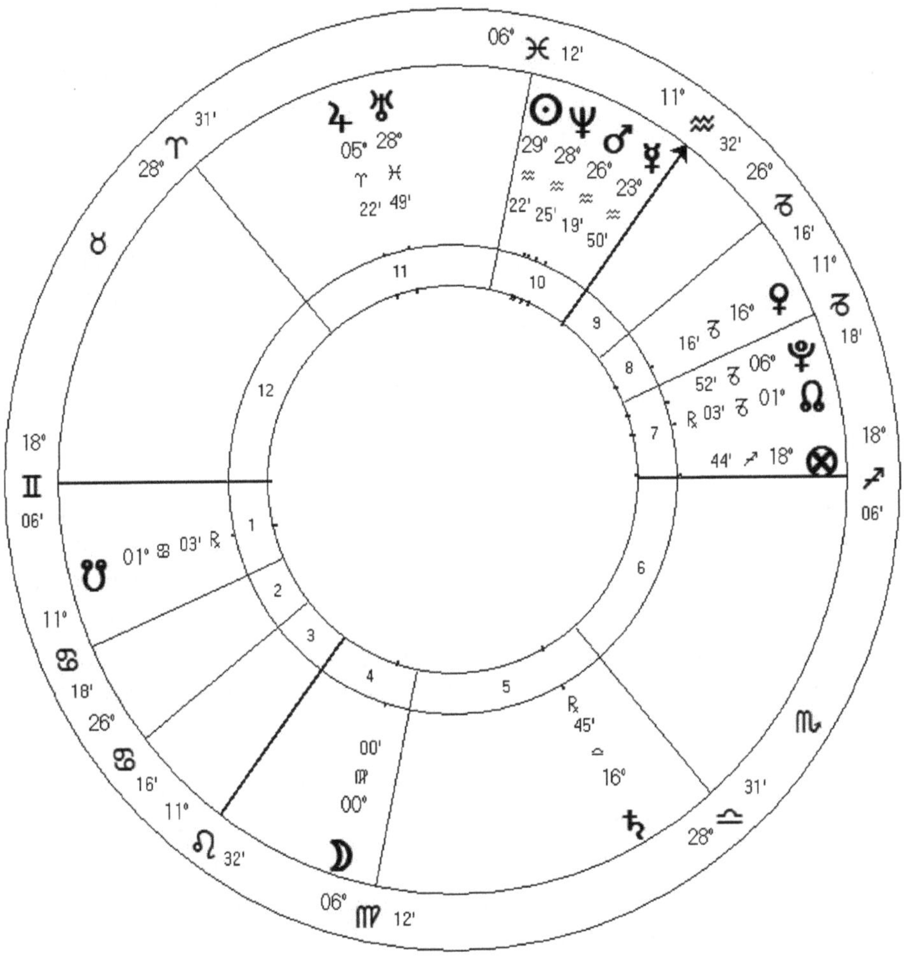

February 18, 2011, 10:40 A.M. | Warsaw, Poland | 18 Gemini

The querent had been suffering from numbness and tingling in her fingers and toes, with bouts of tingling and tremor in her legs. Her doctor thought this was the early stages of multiple sclerosis. She was waiting to see a neurologist, but this would take some weeks. She asked, “Have I got multiple sclerosis? If not, is it some other serious illness? If it is MS, will it progress quickly?”

Medical questions demand the utmost caution. I am appalled at the carelessness with which some will diagnose and prescribe despite lacking any medical knowledge. Astrology alone is not enough! Yet if we are aware of our limitations and do not presume to step beyond them, much of value can be done.

The astrologer is rarely the first port of call when someone falls ill. It is this that allows judgement, because we are not being asked to make the primary diagnosis. The testimonies in the chart might sound to me like disease A, but for all I, in my ignorance of medicine, know they could as well fit disease B, C, D, E or F. But in most cases we are being asked not to make the diagnosis ourselves, but, as here, to check a diagnosis already given. So we can, with all due caution, suggest "Yes, the chart supports what your doctor has told you" or "No, it doesn't look like that: maybe you should have some more tests", all the while stressing that this is a lay-person's understanding of an astrological chart, not the opinion of a medical expert. Yet time after time the client will report back after a few weeks, saying "I've had more tests, and they've confirmed what the chart showed".

The querent is signified by Mercury, ruler of the 1st house. Don't use the Moon as cosignificator of the querent in medical questions: give the querents more than one planet and you'll find they are all suffering from every illness known to man. The nature of Mercury is cold and dry. Here, it is in Aquarius, a hot/moist sign. The incompatibility between Mercury's own nature and the nature of the sign it is in points us towards Saturn, the ruler of that sign, as significator of the illness.

An afflicting planet can also signify the illness instead of or as well as the ruler of the sign. Mars is close to Mercury here. Had Mercury been separating from its conjunction with Mars, Mars could show the problem. But with over 2 degrees between them and the aspect not yet perfected it is too far away to be significant here.

Once we have the significator of the illness, we can refer to Richard Saunders (see Glossary) to find what he says about it. In the diagnostic section of his book, he gives the humoral imbalance shown by each planet in each sign, and lists some typical manifestations of this imbalance. Saturn in the middle of Libra, he says, is hot and moist. But multiple sclerosis is not a hot/moist illness. It is cold and dry, a closing down of nervous function through an excess of melancholy, the cold/dry humour. This argues against the illness being multiple sclerosis.

Saturn is, however, tied in closely by exact aspect and mutual reception with Venus. Venus in the middle of Capricorn, Saunders says, is cold and dry, with a particular propensity for bringing problems in the legs. This close association of the two planets suggests that while the illness (Saturn) is not MS, it is producing symptoms similar to it. Saturn is in the 5th house, which shows the liver and associated organs. This suggests that rather than MS, the problem could be the body's inability to assimilate nutrients efficiently.

Some time later the client wrote that she had seen the specialist, who had given her an MRI scan which showed she did not have multiple sclerosis. Blood tests had revealed that her body was creating antibodies that were preventing her absorbing vitamin B12. Taking high doses of B12 had made her symptoms all but disappear.

Will My Dog Get Better? Will It Survive?

Fotini Christodoulou

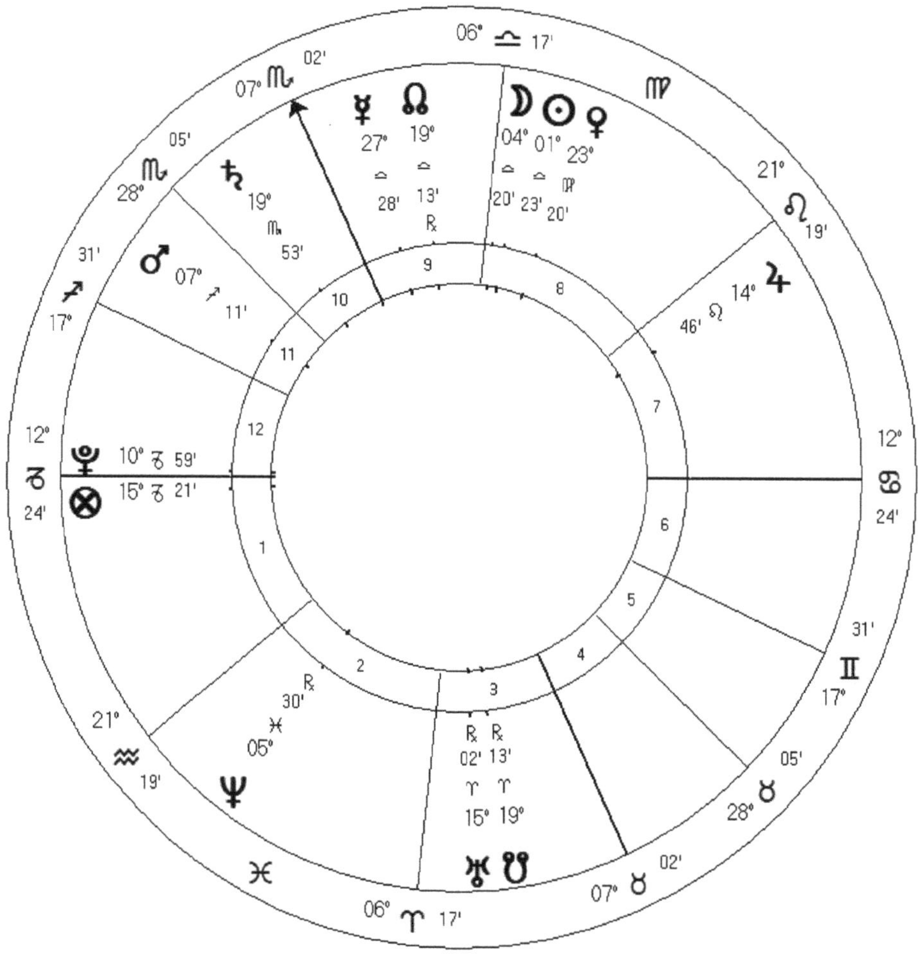

September 24, 2014, 3:34 P.M. | Thessaloniki, Greece | 12 Capricorn

The querent's aged dog was in a bad way and she was very worried about whether its condition would improve and if it would survive. The vet hadn't given her satisfactory information about the problem, except the fact that the problem was likely located in the intestines and had suggested a special diet and medicines.

The querent's dog is represented by Lord 6, Mercury. It is a cold and dry planet in a hot and moist sign (Libra): which only confirms that the dog is ill. It is disposited by Venus which is the significator of the illness. Venus in Virgo according to *Saunders* causes illness and pains of the bowel and navel – intestines and stomach. Which confirms the vet's suspicions and therefore the treatment he had suggested was appropriate.

Will it survive? To answer that part of the query we must check both the radical and turned Lords 8 (death), which in this case is the Sun and Saturn. Mercury doesn't form an aspect to neither of them. The dog will survive.

Will it get better? Mercury has been in a mutual reception with the significator of the illness for a long time, so this problem has been with the dog for a long time. The querent confirmed that the dog had chewed on some plastic trash about a year ago and she wasn't able to stop him before eating a part of it. It was unwell the next day but it soon was back to normal and so she wasn't alarmed.

Mercury will break this reception in a bit less than 3 units of time, so this should show it getting better – as it stops being ruled by the significator of the illness, the illness will still be ruled by it and the dog will enter the illness detriment. This suggests that while the damage was done and it is there (Venus), the dog manages to overcome it. It was judged that it would get better in about 3 days.

The chart was confirmed.

Will Zaza Recover?

Kathryn Silvestre

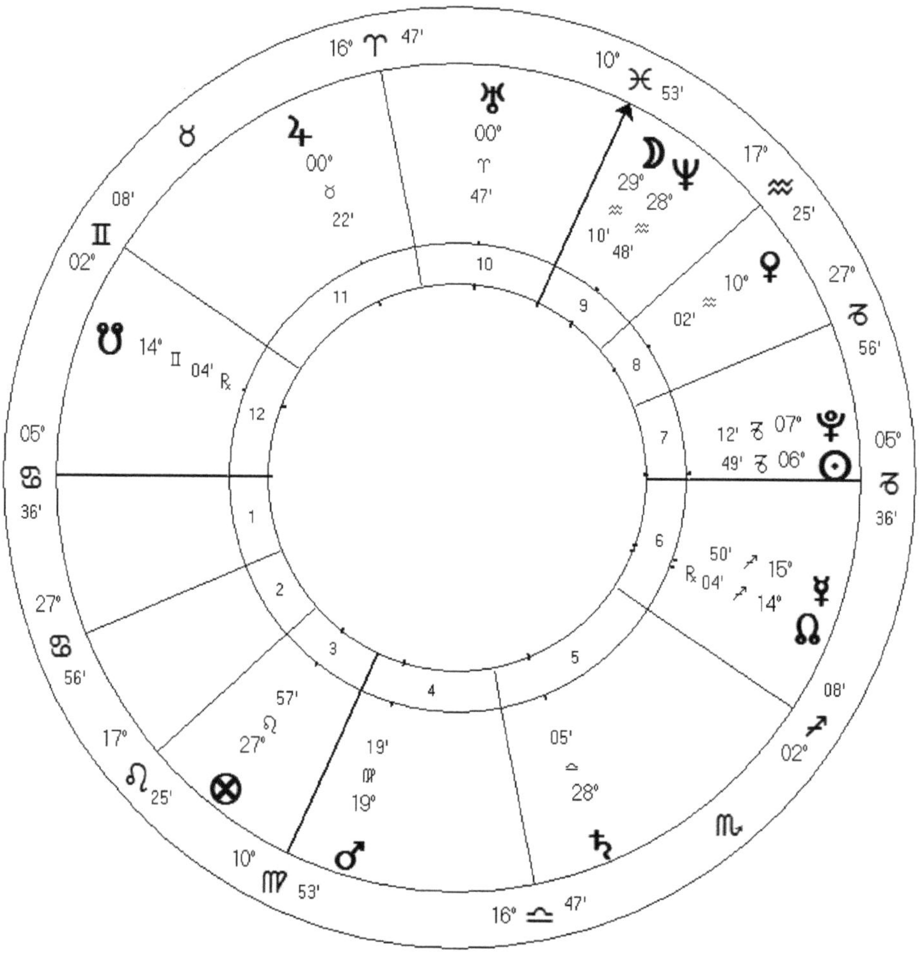

December 28, 2011, 4:13 P.M. | Milwaukee, WI | 5 Cancer

My beloved elderly cat became ill just after Christmas in 2011, requiring an overnight stay in the animal hospital. She'd had a "vestibular episode", we later learned, meaning she couldn't stay upright or walk without falling over. When we brought her home, she wasn't herself: we almost didn't recognize her. I was fearful she would die.

Although the question is phrased as you see it above, essentially my question was, "Will Zaza die from this?"

Animals smaller than goats are signified by the 6th house in astrology. The sign on the cusp of the sixth is Sagittarius, making Jupiter my cat's significator. I am the Moon, though my planet is not needed to reach judgment. As you will see in a moment, there is a more important role for the Moon.

In horaries concerning the death of someone other than the querent, we check both the radical 8th house (death) and the turned 8th house from the house in question (the death of that specific person or thing).

Capricorn is the sign on cusp 8, making Saturn Lord 8. The 8th house from the sixth is the 1st house. With Cancer on the 1st cusp, the Moon is turned Lord 8. In order to find out if Zaza will live, then, we must check whether there is an applying aspect between Jupiter and either Saturn or the Moon.

Jupiter is newly in Taurus. There is no applying aspect with either of the two planets that could signify death in this chart. Saturn is at 28:05 Libra; no aspect is possible from there with a planet in early Taurus, because the signs do not behold each other. Nor does the Moon, at 29 Aquarius, aspect Jupiter from within its current sign. The Moon opposes Jupiter by antiscion, but for death we must have a bodily aspect; the antiscion won't kill. The Moon will complete a sextile with Jupiter once it moves into Pisces, but that does not count: we would need an aspect within the current sign to show death, and there is none. Therefore, Zaza will live! And so she did.

What else is worth noting in this chart? Jupiter has just moved from Aries into Taurus. The important thing about this is that it shows us "something has just changed". We know what that change is: she was just ill, and that illness has changed her.

What does Jupiter's being in Taurus mean, in this context? In medical questions we look at the qualities of the sign a planet is in – meaning temperature and moisture – to see if these qualities match the natural qualities of the planet in question. Jupiter is by nature a warm and moist planet. Jupiter had recently been in Aries, which is a hot and dry sign. Jupiter shares heat with Aries, which is something. However, Jupiter shares neither heat nor moisture with Taurus, because Taurus, being an earth sign, is cold and dry. So Jupiter in Taurus shows Zaza's overall condition has worsened, though it is not immediately life-threatening. Taurus is also a fixed sign, suggesting that Zaza's condition, though not great, is at least stable. Being at zero degrees, this stable condition will last for a long while.

And so it was. Although we never discovered the root cause of Zaza's vestibular episode, a shot of cortisone enabled her full recovery in the short-term. Thereafter, a small dose of this medication twice daily kept her stable, allowing us to continue enjoying her company until she passed away peacefully at home two years later.

Will Grandfather Survive This Time?

Fotini Christodoulou

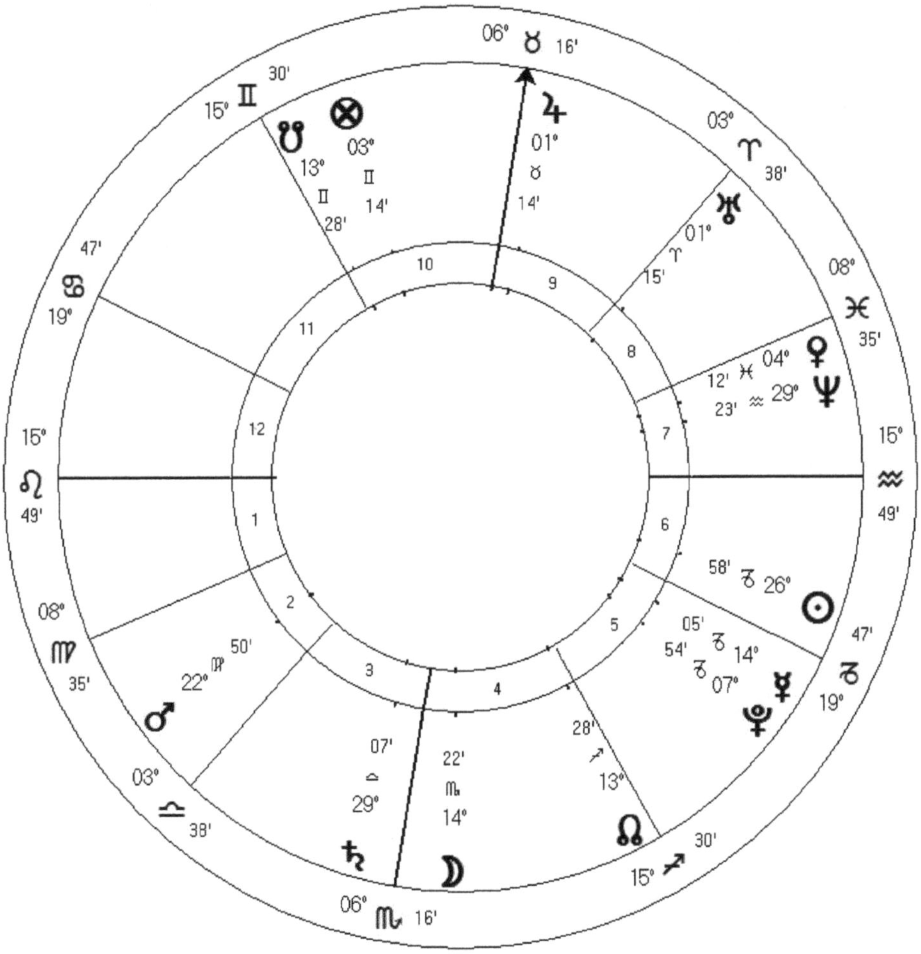

January 17, 2012, 6:58 P.M. | Thessaloniki, Greece | 15 Leo

The querent's grandfather (on mother's side) had been in and out of hospital for months as he started dealing with multiple health issues further burdening his already compromised health problem and fragile physical condition. The doctors said to the family that the odds were against him and that he wouldn't be able to make it this time. This is a straight forward question about death. The querent is not asking about diagnosis or about the development of the illness: all they want to know is if their loved one will survive this particular time.

As mentioned the question is about the querent's grandfather from the mother's side: that brings us back to the radical 1st house (4th of the 10th), so Lord 1 is the Sun. That is not a problem as we don't need the querent in this chart. Death is signified by the 8th house and its lord. Consequently, the radical and turned 8th is the same and its lord is Jupiter.

In this case we hope there isn't a dangerous change in our significator's condition and that Lord 1 doesn't aspect Lord 8 or that this aspect is somehow prohibited.

The Sun, Lord 1, is located at 26:58 Capricorn, close to entering its own detriment – well describing the situation the doctors have mentioned to the family. Jupiter, Lord 8, has just entered Taurus. Therefore they cannot form an aspect. The Sun's immediate next aspect will be a square to Saturn right at the edge of leaving Capricorn, which means that the contact with Lord 8, Jupiter, is prohibited: grandfather will survive this one. And so it proved.

Lost & Found

Where Is My ATM Card?

Leah Cuperman

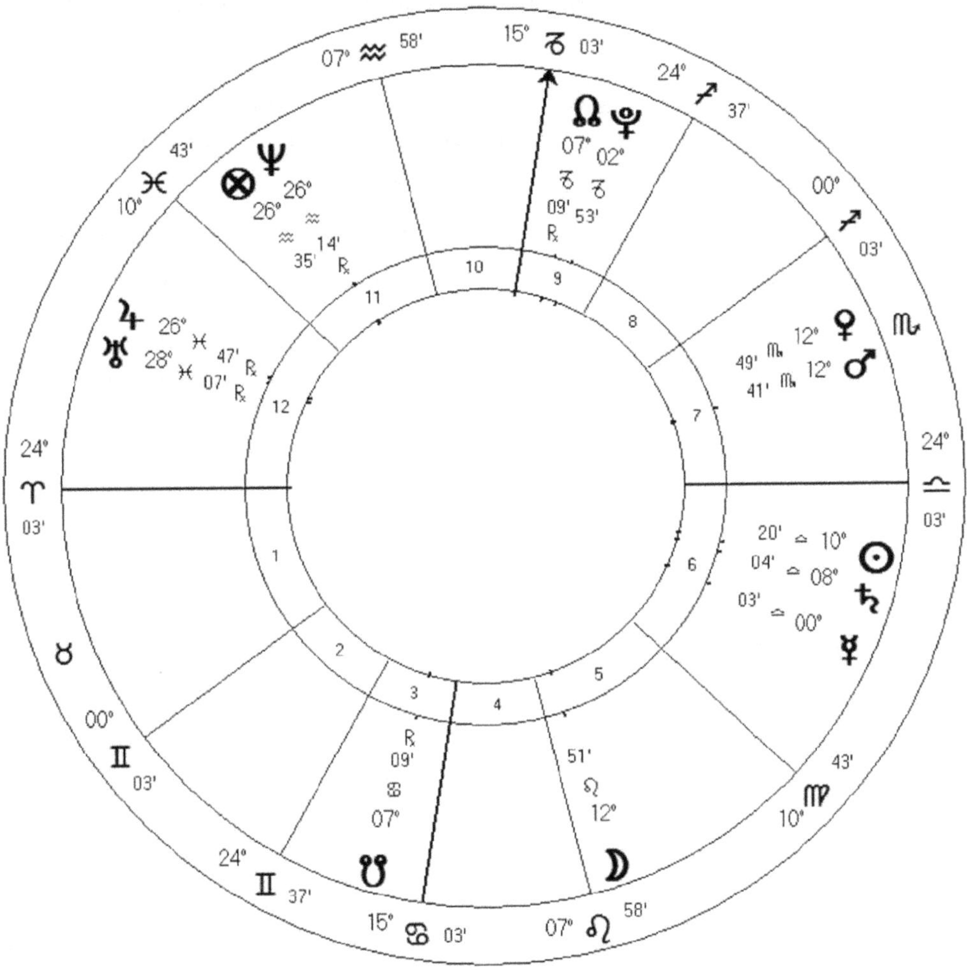

October 03, 2010, 5:57 P.M. | Herzliya, Israel | 24 Aries

My friend had lost her ATM card. She remembered using it for the last time in a shop, but was sure she had got it back from the cashier, along with the receipt. Next day, she couldn't find the card.

She asked: "Where is my ATM card? "

My friend, as the querent, is signified by the first house, which is ruled by Mars at 12:41 Scorpio. Her possession, the card, is signified by the 2nd house, ruled by Mercury at 0:03 Libra. In many questions about lost money, cards, or documents we often use Mercury anyway, as natural ruler, whether it rules the 2nd house or not.

So where is the card? Mercury has just entered Libra, a Venus sign, meaning the card is with something related to the nature of Venus – which could be clothes.

Libra is an airy sign, showing that the card is high up on a shelf, or close to a window or a TV. These are good clues, but the chart is able to give us a still better description to narrow down the options.

If the Venus sign points us towards clothes, the condition of Venus will describe those clothes. Venus is in its detriment: they are dirty clothes.

As advised, my friend went to her laundry basket, which is next to a window, and found her card in a pocket of the jeans she had worn the previous day.

Where Is My Scarf?

Molly Morrissey

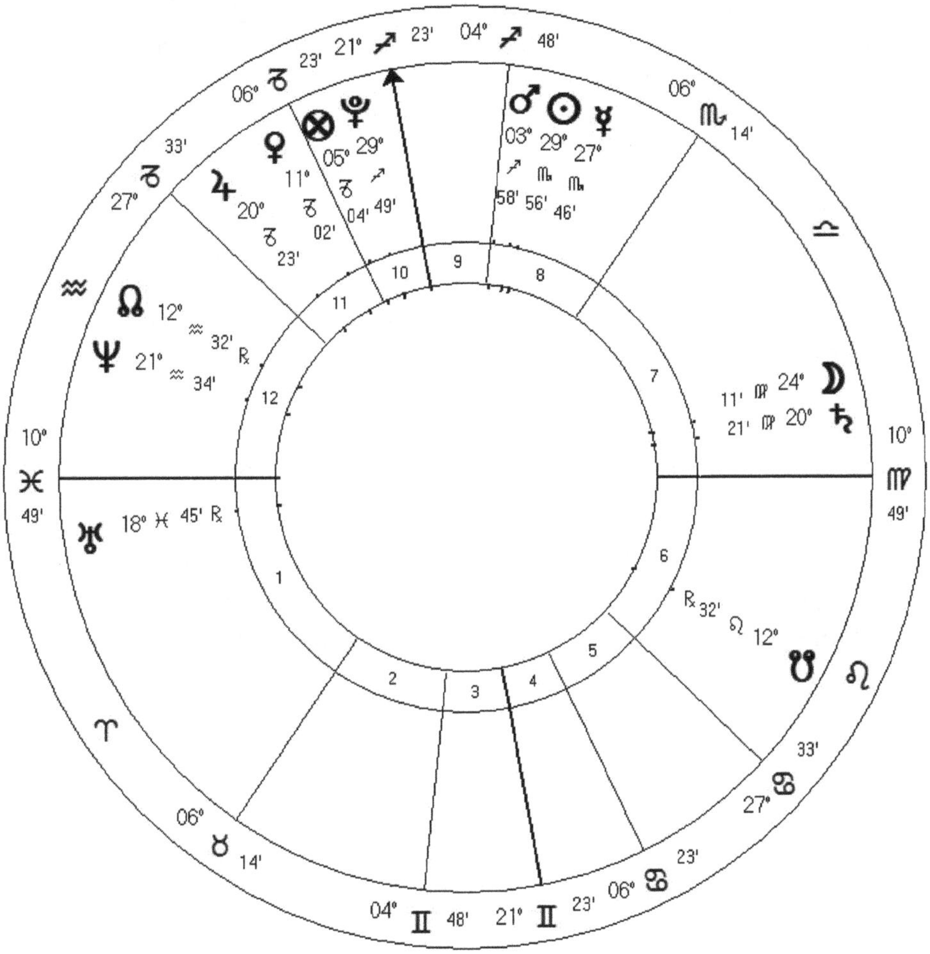

November 21, 2008, 1:26 P.M. | Redmond, WA | 10 Pisces

I realized I couldn't find my favorite fluffy white scarf anywhere. Not one to lose things, I panicked a little but then realized this would be the perfect opportunity to cast my first horary chart.

Since I am considering an inanimate object, the object would be represented either by the second house or the fourth, whichever fits better.

With Taurus on the cusp of the second house, I'm taking Venus to signify the scarf, that planet being very appropriate for a fluffy, soft scarf. With Mercury being the other choice, Venus is clearly the better fit.

Venus sits in the 11th house. The scarf is with a friend. I had just moved a month before the scarf was lost and was not sure if I was coming or going. I could not remember having been anywhere with the scarf when I discovered it gone, though I had remembered unpacking it. When I cast the chart, I thought it was ridiculous, since I couldn't remember having been to see anyone recently.

I, as the querent, am signified by Jupiter and the Moon. Both of my signifiers are separating from aspects with Lord 11, Saturn, a friend. We don't need this testimony, though at the time, it did confirm that I'd been to see someone, though I couldn't think of who it could be.

With a lost object chart, we do not necessarily need an aspect for recovery. It would be questionable to see the impending conjunction of Venus and Jupiter as confirmation of my getting the scarf back since the conjunction is prohibited by the impending Venus/Saturn trine. Lost object charts also don't usually show timing, since the location of the object usually sends the querent off on the chase.

After checking my calendar, I saw that I had, indeed, been to see a friend. A phone call proved she had the scarf and I got it back about a week or so later. An eloquent start to my investigation of horary astrology.

Where Is the Tape?

Leah Cuperman

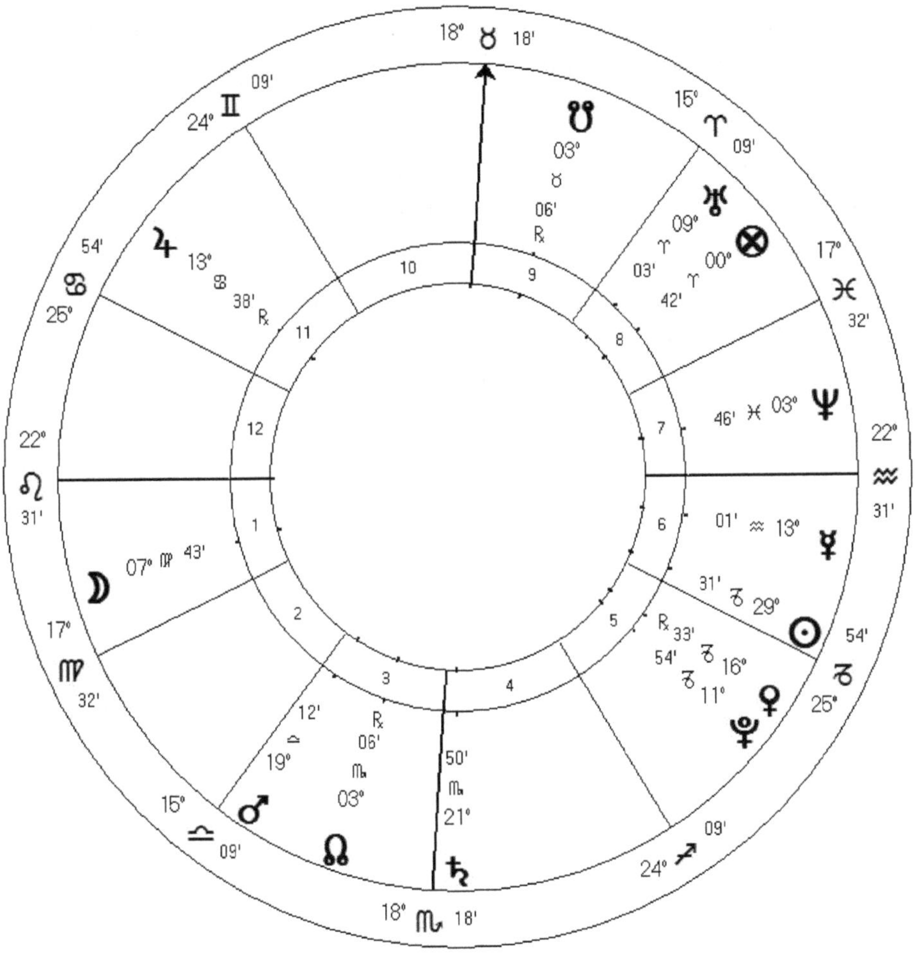

January 19, 2014, 6:48 P.M. | Herzliya, Israel | 22 Leo

This was my own question. A friend was collecting information for a book he was writing. I had a tape containing interviews that would be useful to him, and after looking for it on my shelves with no success, I decided to cast a chart with the question: "Where is the tape?"

As a belonging that can be moved around, the tape is signified by Lord 2, Mercury, at 13:01 Aquarius.

I was sure I hadn't lent the tape to anyone, so it had to be at home. The house where Mercury, the significator of the tape, is located will show where in the house it can be found. Mercury is in the 6th house. Even though I don't have any servants, the 6th house still shows the "servants' areas": the first clue.

Second clue: Mercury is in Aquarius, an air sign. Air signs tell us that the missing object is somewhere high up, on a shelf, or maybe by a window or close to a TV.

The third clue: Mercury is in Aquarius, meaning the tape must be with something of the nature of Saturn, which would suggest meanings such as old, dark, or heavy.

The servants' areas in my flat are limited: just a small closet where I keep the vacuum cleaner and a toolbox. On the shelves at the top of this closet are some ancient photo albums and a bag with negatives. The tape was right next to these albums and the negatives.

Where's My Passport?

John Frawley

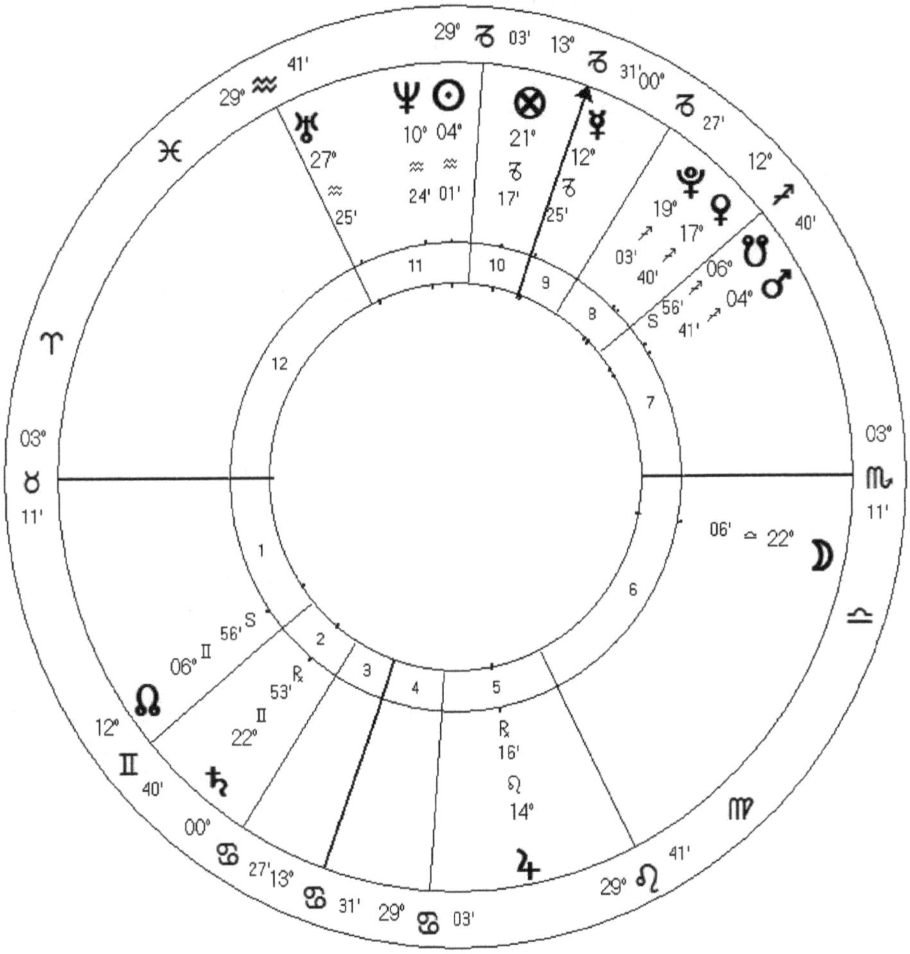

January 24, 2003, 10:46 A.M. | London, England | 3 Taurus

A friend phoned. "Help! I'm flying abroad this afternoon, but I can't find my passport. Where is it? Will I find it on time?"

The querent is shown by Venus, ruler of the 1st house. A lost object can be shown by whichever of Lord 2 or Lord 4 describes it better, or by any other planet that gives a particularly close description of the object. A passport is a document, so we can take Lord 2, which is Mercury, as its significator. The placement of Mercury will tell us where the passport is.

A planet within about 5 degrees of the next house-cusp, and in the same sign as that cusp, is considered as being in that next house. So Mercury is in the 10th house. Each house can show many possible locations. Among others, the 10th could show her workplace, or her mother's home; it could be the formal room of her own house, or the attic; even her husband's father's home.

Common sense gives us a hierarchy of probability, depending upon the nature of the missing object. If we were looking for Granddad's medals, the attic might be a likely place; much less so for a passport. I knew my friend worked from home, so her home office would be a likely location. The 10th could also show a place of work outside the home, but this is less likely: if she went out to work, we might have taken the formal room as our first choice. Similarly, a passport is more likely to be somewhere in her own home than at her Mum's.

The chart provides another clue. Mercury and Venus are conjunct by antiscion. The conjunction is separating, so it cannot be taken as evidence of finding the object, but it does show that it is very close to her. This, of course, increases the likelihood of its being found and found quickly, but it also allows us to rule out any location that is not close to her – in this case, any location outside her own home.

We can run with the idea that it is in her home office, check that out, and if it doesn't prove correct move on to the next place in the hierarchy of probability. Mercury is right on the cusp of the house, so the passport will be close to the door of the room. It is in an earth sign, so the passport will be on the ground, or close to it. And so it proved: the passport was on the floor by the door of her home office.

But will she find it in time for her flight? Testimony of finding the object is usually superfluous. If, as here, we have an exact location we can send the querent to look in that location without scratching our head over whether the chart confirms recovery. Many such charts seem not to bother providing such testimony. But here we have it.

She needs the passport in order to travel: she cannot make the journey without it. The Moon, the querent's cosignificator, makes an immediate aspect with Saturn, ruler of the 9th, the house of long journeys. This shows that she makes the journey, so she must find the passport. The aspect is a trine, so there is no delay, and it perfects in less than 1 degree. In a lost object horary, timing from an aspect perfecting in less than 1 degree can always be read as "more or less immediately". So she will not need to rebook for a later flight, so she must find the passport very quickly. The chart was judged and passport found within 10 minutes of her asking the question. Not, I stress, through any great cleverness on the part of the astrologer, but from the application of a few simple rules.

Where's My Notebook?

Kathryn Silvestre

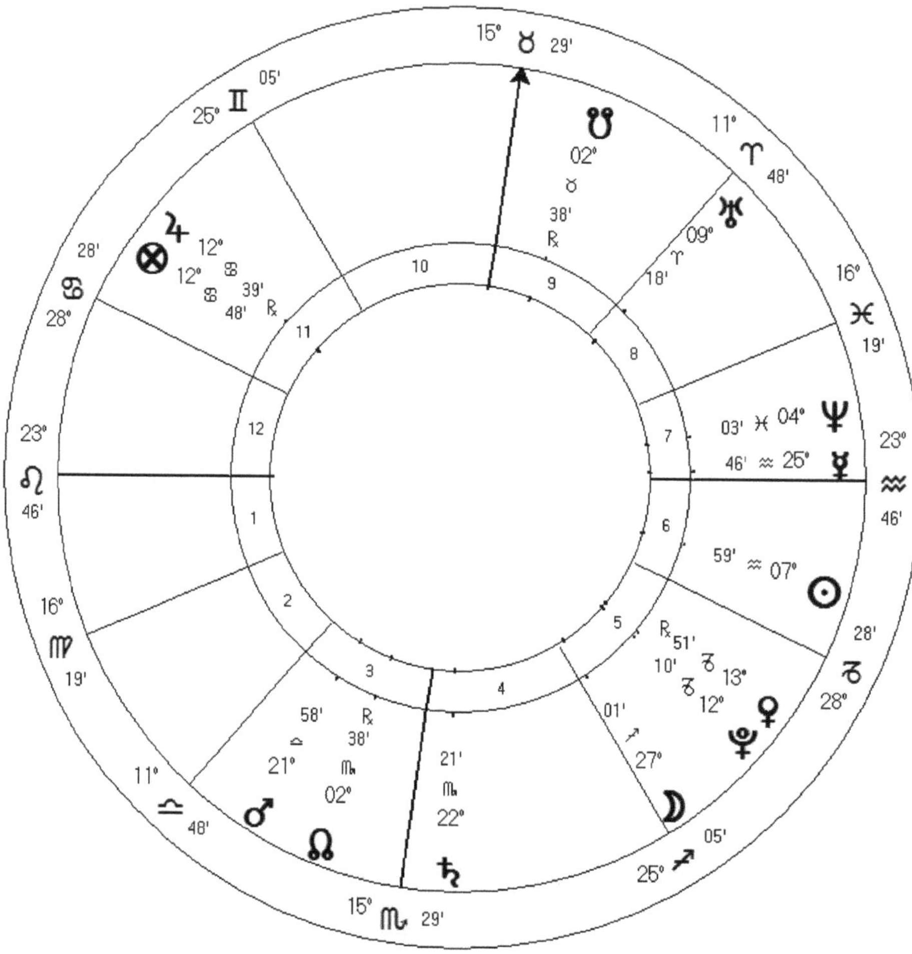

January 27, 2014, 6:15 P.M. | Milwaukee, WI | 23 Leo

Lost object horaries can be tricky, so it's always a pleasure when they work just as they're supposed to. This is one such chart.

The querent had been looking for a notebook. It was **The Notebook**, containing vital material from her doctoral studies, completed a decade earlier. Both she and her husband had searched their house but could not find it.

First we must identify the key significators needed to reach judgment. Our querent is Lord 1, the Sun, the planet ruling the sign on the Ascendant

(Leo). What is the notebook? For lost object horaries we take either Lord 2 or Lord 4, whichever better fits the object by description. The obvious choice here is Lord 2, Mercury, ruler of the sign on the second cusp (Virgo). Mercury rules little things (like letters of the alphabet) and all forms of communication: perfect for a notebook!

Where is Mercury? It is in the seventh house, close to the Descendant – two degrees exactly. Even three degrees would be "close"; more than that, likely not. That Mercury is close to the Descendant tells us that the notebook is close by. Mercury's placement in the seventh is also telling us where the object is. The seventh is the house of the querent's partner, in this case her husband. This tells us clearly it is "with hubby's stuff". Great!

Do we need an aspect showing recovery? Not always. In this case, we have a clear location – with hubby's stuff – so we know there's a good chance of recovery. There is no applying aspect between either of the querent's significators – the Sun or the Moon – and the object, Mercury, in this chart, but I was not discouraged by that. There is a separating aspect between the Moon and Mercury. As both the querent and her hubby had already looked for the notebook, this separating aspect suggests they have come across it already but just didn't see it.

I told the querent to look again among hubby's things. She did, and soon after, found the notebook in one of his boxes, in the basement. Success!

Where does the basement fit in? In lost object horaries we can use the significator's dispositor for further details on the location of the object. We know the notebook is with hubby's things because Mercury is in the seventh. But where among hubby's things? There could be several places where he keeps his stuff (the bedroom, the office, etc.). Mercury is in Aquarius, which is ruled by Saturn, so we look at Saturn's placement for the next clue. Saturn is in the fourth house. As the lowest house in the chart, this is the basement.

Where is my pendant? Did I misplace it or was it stolen?

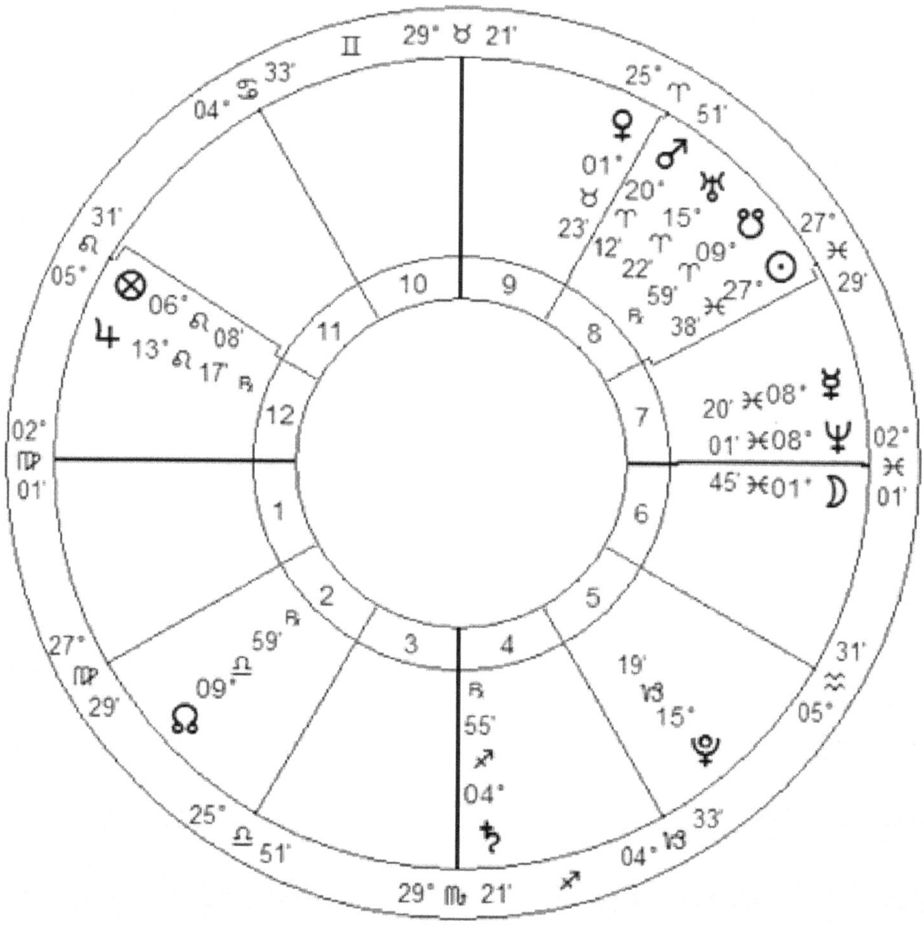

March 18, 2015, 3:46 P.M. | Herzliya, Israel | 2 Virgo

After spending some time looking unsuccessfully for her rose quartz pendant, this client started wondering if she had simply misplaced it, or if her cleaning lady had stolen it. She asked: “Where is my pendant? Did I misplace it or was it stolen by my cleaner?”

In this chart, the missing pendant is signified by Lord 2, Mercury at 8:20 Pisces. The cleaning lady, as an employee of the querent, is signified by Lord 6, Saturn Rx at 4:55 Sagittarius. Mercury has recently separated from an aspect with Saturn, which could be a testimony of theft. However, if the pendant had been stolen by the cleaner, it is most likely that in the chart we would have found Mercury just inside the 6th house, showing that the pendant is with the cleaner.

Mercury is in the 7th house, which in a home signifies the querent's bedroom and/or her husband's place in the home. It is also in the water sign of Pisces, a testimony that the pendant is with something related to water, and is conjunct Neptune, which signifies the turbulent waters of the ocean. Being in one of the mutable signs that is Pisces shows that the pendant is most likely inside something, whether it is a drawer, a box, a bag, etc.

In this chart, Mercury is also Lord 1, and so it has a second role as the significator of the querent. However, because it is already busy signifying the pendant, we can take the Moon to signify the querent. The Moon at 1:45 Pisces is on its way to conjunct Mercury, bringing querent and pendant together, but before this happens, the Moon bumps into Saturn. The only way the querent can reach the pendant is by removing this prohibition by Saturn.

I told the querent that the cleaning lady didn't steal the pendant, and suggested she had a diplomatic word with her, asking her if perhaps she had put it in another place in the house.

After the client got my answer, she decided to look again before talking to the cleaning lady. She found the pendant in her bedroom, inside a small bag she always takes to the beach. It was not until she removed the prohibition from Saturn that she found the pendant: the thought that the cleaner had taken it was preventing her from looking for it herself.

Miscellaneous

Are the Electrical Parts I Bought Fake or Original?

Leah Cuperman

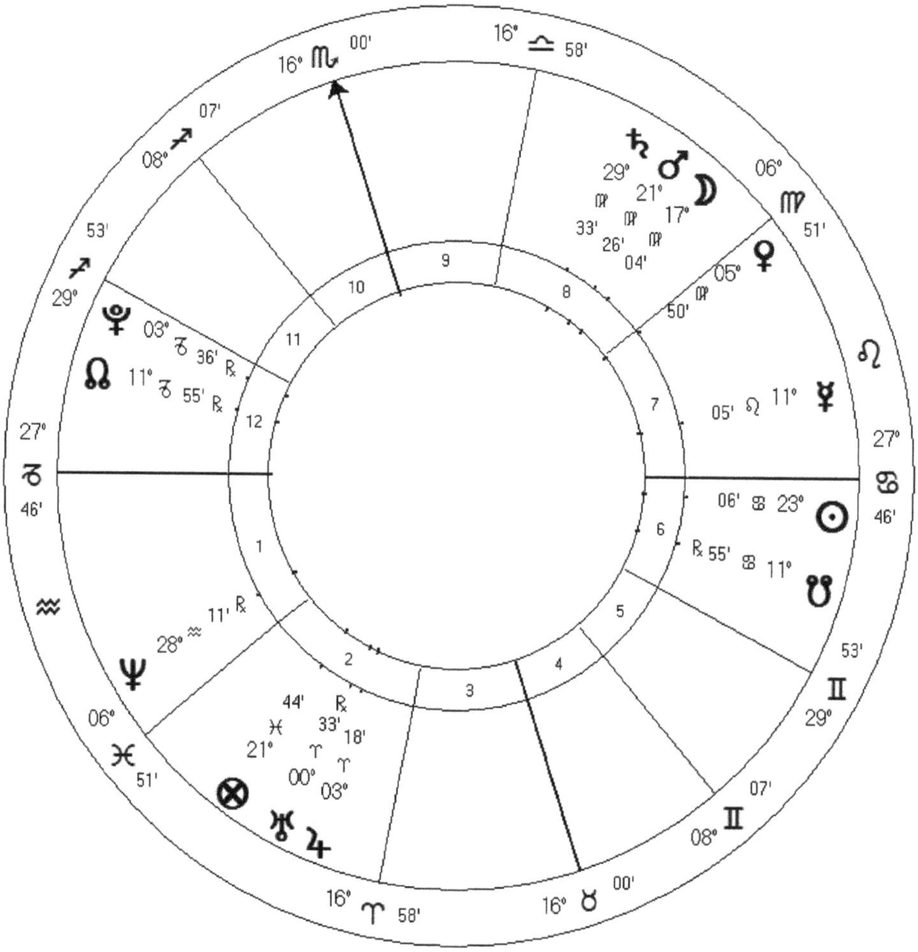

July 15, 2010, 8:01 P.M. | Herzliya, Israel | 27 Capricorn

After placing the order with a salesperson she never previously dealt with, something raised the client's suspicion that the parts she had just purchased might be fake and not work properly.

She asked: "Are the electrical parts I bought fake or original?"

As always, the querent is signified by Lord 1.

The product that the supplier sells is signified by the radical 8th house or turned 2nd house from the 7th, which is ruled by Mercury at 11:05 Leo.

Mercury shows the parts, so we would like to see Mercury being what it really ought to be. This would be shown by it having a lot of essential dignity, conforming to its own true nature. Mercury here has some dignity, by term, but this is very minor. This suggests that the parts are not totally useless, but they are certainly not what they should be.

Furthermore, there is a planet afflicting the radical 8th house (the product from the supplier). Venus at 5:50 Virgo is in its fall, which is a big warning sign that the product is not good.

After a few weeks, the parts arrived and the querent confirmed they were not original.

Will Britain Join the Euro?

John Frawley

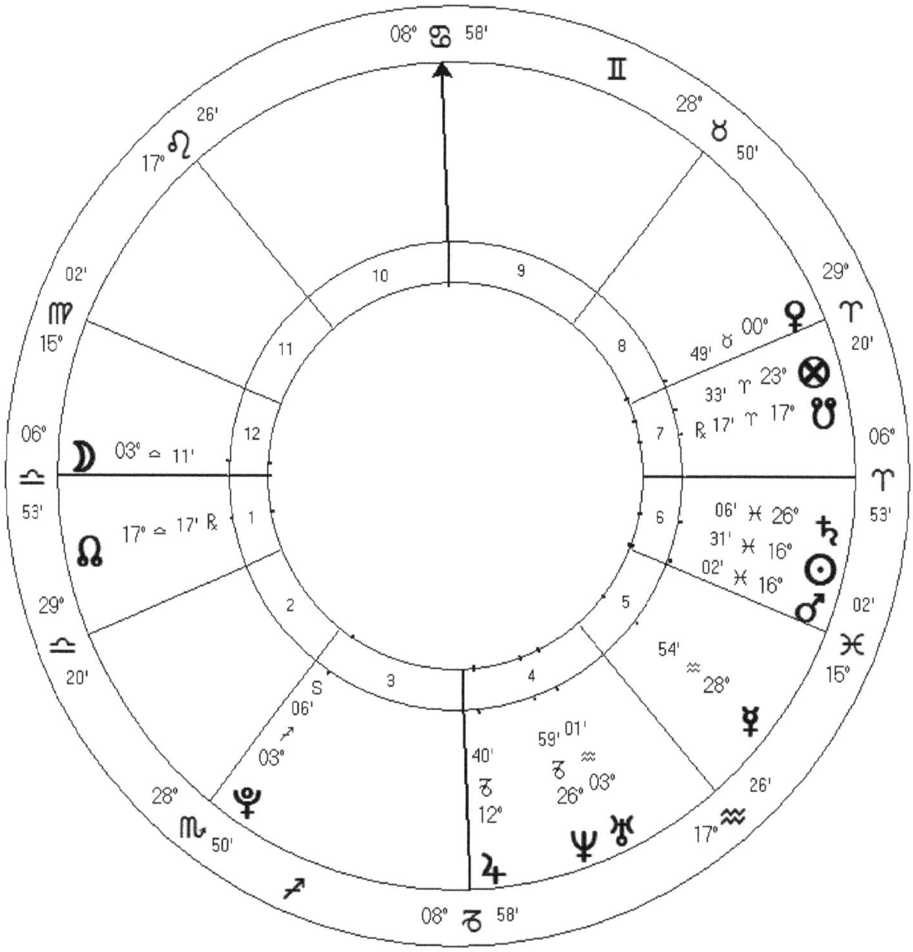

March 06, 1996, 7:40 P.M. | London, England | 6 Libra

There was much talk of Britain adopting the Euro as its currency.

This question raises the issue of caring. There must be a certain level of spontaneous, genuine, concern with the subject of the question if the chart is to provide a sound answer. This does not mean the subject needs to be one of widespread significance: I care whether the cat comes home far more than I do about most things on the front page of the newspaper. But an instant's flickering interest in an item on the TV news or the student astrologer's "Hmmm... what can I ask about now?" is not sufficient.

With questions on financial matters, whatever concern the querent has is usually personal. The interest is not in whether the currency will rise or fall, but in whatever impact this will have on the querent's own investments. If the interest is personal, it is this personal interest that should be the subject of the question. Consider: I might think that the currency rising will make me rich, so I ask if the currency will rise. Perhaps it will rise, and perhaps this will have the positive effect I anticipate on my finances. But this could be outweighed by some other event, so I go bust. I have not received the relevant answer because I have not asked the question that concerns me.

For this reason, abstract questions about the financial markets, such as the one asked here, are comparatively rare. This querent, however, shared the common English belief that joining the Euro today meant the Tricolor flying over Buckingham Palace tomorrow. This horrifying thought was quite sufficient grounds for asking the abstract question.

The querent is British, so Britain can be taken as 1st house: "us". There is a process of selection involved in whether Britain will be accepted to the Euro-zone, but this does not mean it is a 10th-house matter, like "Will I get the job?" Many questions, such as "Will she go out with me?" involve a process of selection; this does not make them 10th-house issues. It could be seen as "Will we join the others?" which would be a 7th-house matter. But Britain had already joined the European Community and so was to some extent a member of the gang already. The most direct route to judgement is to see this as "Will our money join their money?" It is the most direct route that should always be taken, else we lose ourselves in elaboration.

Our money is shown by the 2nd house, and so is signified by Venus. The other people's money is 2nd house from the 7th, which is the radical 8th house. This is ruled by Mars. At 0 Taurus, Venus has just left the sign of Mars and entered its own sign, a strong indication that the flirtation is already over: what interest there was in joining is gone.

Even so, an aspect between Venus and Mars could give a Yes. Venus applies to sextile Mars, but before that aspect is made it will trine Jupiter. The aspect to Jupiter prohibits any further aspect it might make: so far as we are concerned the sextile to Mars will never happen. If there were an aspect between Venus and Mars we would need to think more about the significance of Venus" change of sign: would this rule out a Yes, or not? But there is no aspect, so that puzzle is only hypothetical.

No aspect, no joining: the judgement is that simple. Judgement does not get any more complicated because the subject is a big one.

What Time Tomorrow Will the Wine Arrive?

Molly Morrissey

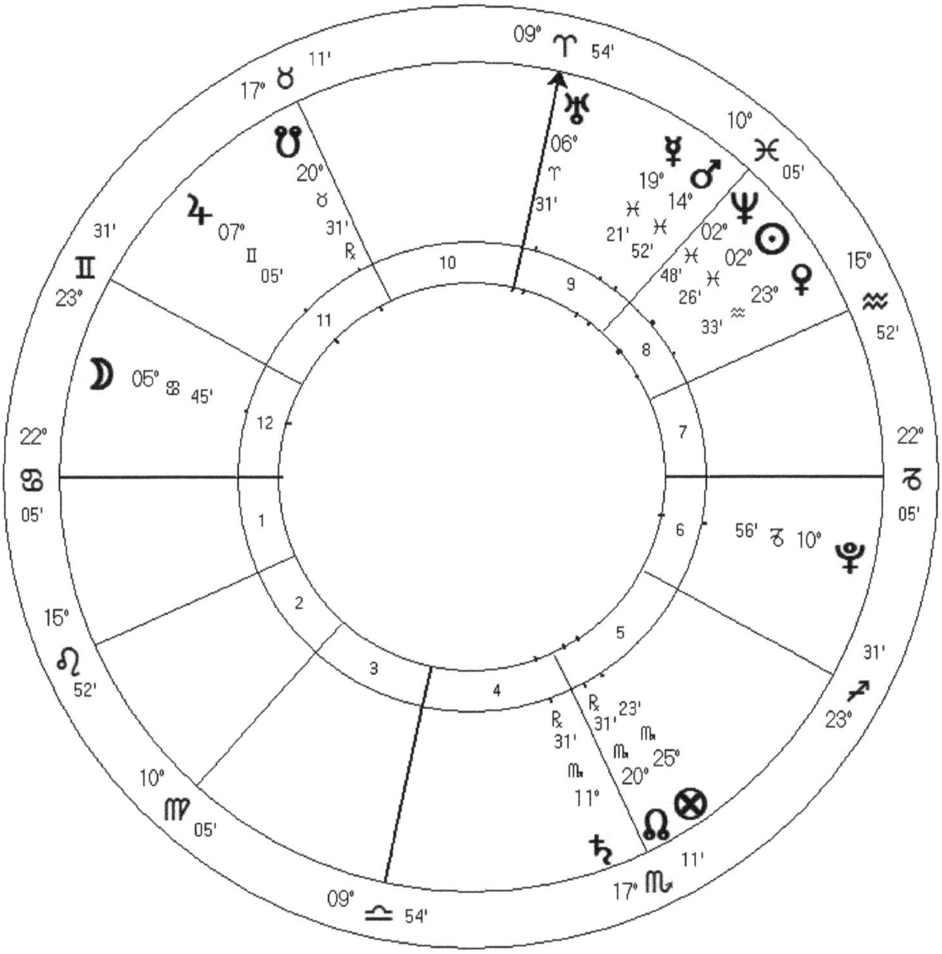

February 20, 2013, 2:21 P.M. | San Diego, CA | 22 Cancer

I had ordered some wine online and they said it would arrive the next day. Ah, the joys of living in the same state as Napa Valley! I called the shipping company and the earliest deliveries they make are 7 am. That is the earliest I could expect the delivery the next day.

I, as the querent, get Lord 1 and the Moon, which are one in the same in this particular chart. I also get Lord 2, Sun, since he signifies my possessions. The people that I am buying the wine from are signified by Lord 7. The package of wine is their possession, signified by Lord 8, Saturn.

The Moon is applying to trine Saturn in about 6 degrees. Hours are the obvious time unit for this question.

The wine will be at my doorstep a little before 1 pm.

And so it proved.

Note: I originally judged this chart thinking the wine was signified by the third from the seventh – the ninth house and Lord 9. Frawley is much clearer on this issue of Letters in the revised *Horary Textbook.* Correspondence are third house, possessions and objects are second house.

When Will the Power-Cut End?

John Frawley

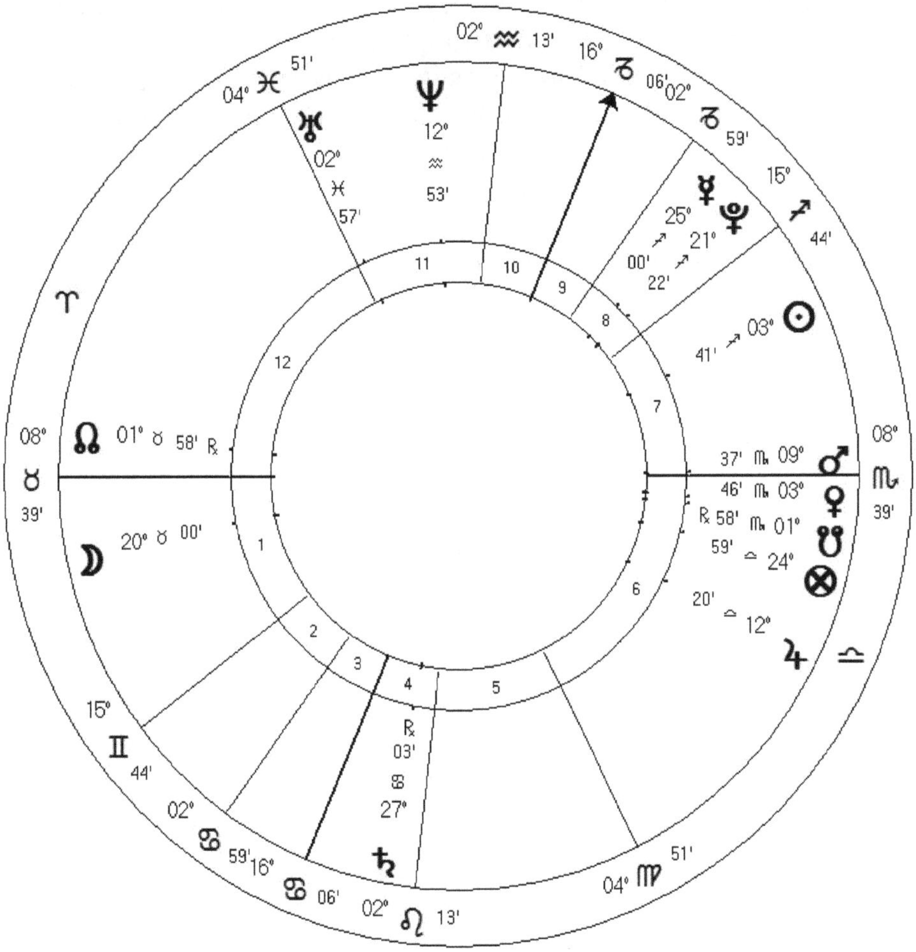

November 25, 2004, 2:50 P.M. | London, England | 8 Taurus

This was my own question – not one of life-changing significance, but nonetheless important to me at the time, as with the power having been off for some while I wanted to know how to arrange my working day. This chart is an illustration of how simple horary can be.

On a November afternoon in London, such a question was much concerned with light, the natural significator of which is the Sun. But I was not asking about natural light. What interested me was artificial light, the kind that we use when the Sun is not providing. That is signified by the Moon, whose job is to shed light in the darkness.

The Moon here is about to rise above the Ascendant, which is the eastern horizon, a literal statement of what I was hoping for: artificial light becoming visible. The timing will be given by the number of degrees it must travel before it rises. This is 11 degrees, so the power will be restored in 11 units of time. My hope that this might be 11 minutes was contradicted by the sign the Moon was in. This is Taurus, a fixed sign, showing the slowest relevant units. When deciding which time-units to use we would usually consider the house the planet is in, too. The Moon is in an angular house, which again would give the slowest units. We cannot consider the house here, though, because doing so would involve us in a circular logic: we are interested in the Moon being about to rise, so it must be in the 1st house, which would make a fast time-unit an impossibility. The sign alone tells that the power will be restored in 11 hours, which is exactly what happened.

Will My Daughter Get the Funded Spot?

Kathryn Silvestre

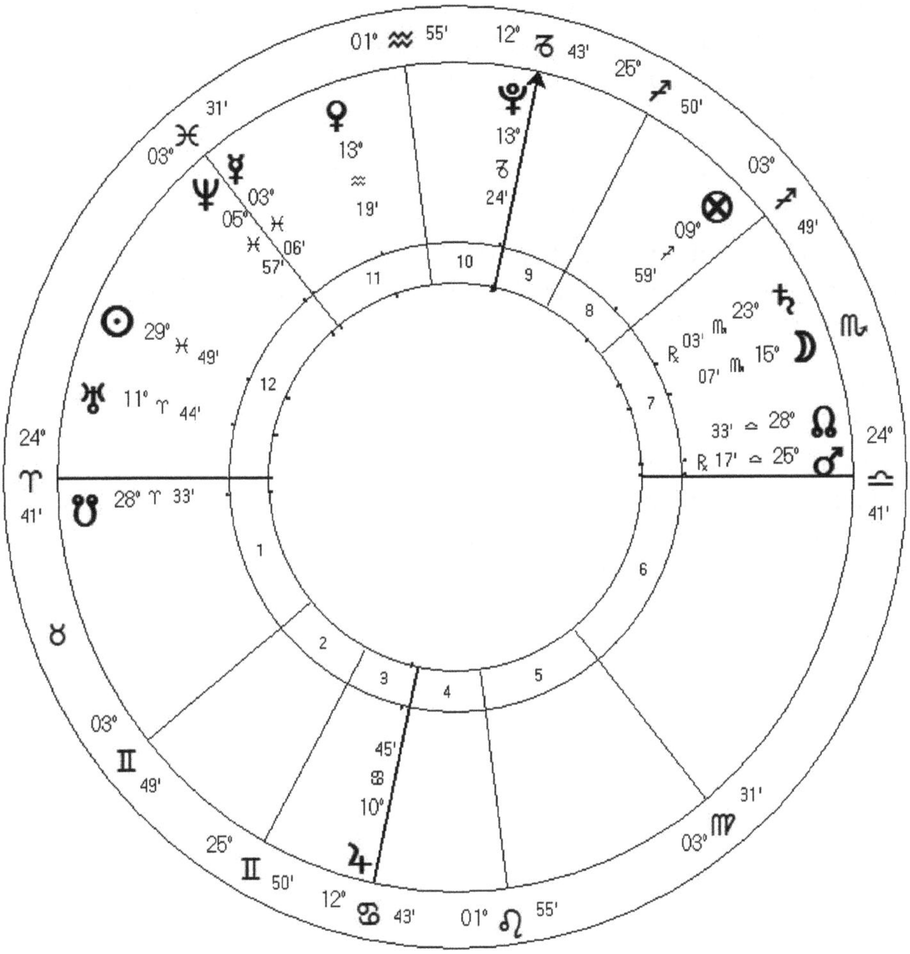

March 20, 2014, 7:55 A.M. | Milwaukee, WI | 24 Aries

Sometimes horary provides the answer to a question in the simplest possible fashion. The more I practice horary, the more this seems to be so. There is a beauty in this simplicity that I've come to love.

The question is mine. I had applied for a funded spot for my daughter at her school. I knew it was possible others had applied for the spot and that it might come down to a lottery. I was worried about the consequences of her not getting chosen; thus the question was born.

When deciding which planet is the key significator in horary, I've found that it's best to use the most straightforward approach. This question involves my daughter (Lord 5), her elementary school (Lord 3), and government funding (Lord 11, as the second from the 10th: the government's money). In essence, though, the question concerns my daughter: Lord 5. Leo is the sign on cusp five, therefore my daughter's significator is the Sun.

The Sun is in Pisces where it has no essential dignity. It is about to move into Aries, the sign of its exaltation: a big improvement. Daughter's condition, in the context of this particular question, is about to change for the better: yes, she'll get the spot! A phone call from the school the next morning confirmed the good news.

The reader may wonder if we don't need an aspect showing the funding coming either to me (Lord Ascendant or the Moon), or to my pocket (Lord 2), or to my daughter. We do have an applying conjunction between the Moon and the significator of the funding, Saturn, ruler of Aquarius on cusp 11. But this is unnecessary for judgment. The immediate improvement in the condition of my daughter's significator provides the answer.

Will the Thief Come Back?

Leah Cuperman

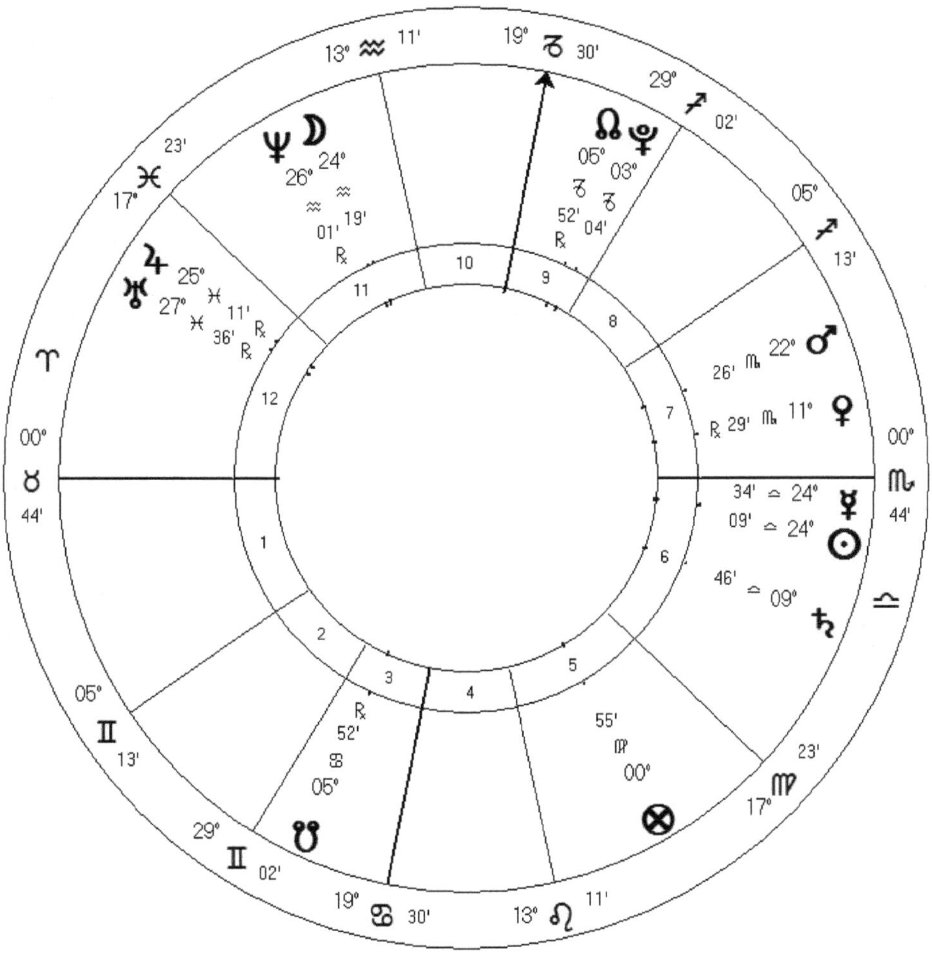

October 17, 2010, 5:21 P.M. | Herzliya, Israel | 0 Taurus

The querent's lawn-mower was stolen from the garden of her house. The video from her security camera showed a man in a truck stopping to take the lawn-mower and then driving off. The querent was afraid that the thief would return to steal something else, perhaps from inside the house. Her question was, "Will the thief come back?"

The querent is signified by Lord 1, Venus (retrograde) at 11:29 Scorpio. There are two types of possessions we may own: the ones we can move around and the ones we can't, such as real estate. Possessions that can be moved around are usually signified by the 2nd house of the chart, and those that cannot, by the 4th. In this case, the lawn-mower is signified by the 2nd house, which in this chart is ruled by Mercury at 24:34 Libra.

Even though the 7th house signifies our open enemies, a thief is not always signified by this house. A person who steals something from you could be anyone: a worker that you hired to do a plumbing job (a 6th house person), a neighbor with sticky fingers (a 3rd house person), and so on. We must keep our eyes open and pay attention to what the chart wants to tell us.

We know the lawn-mower was stolen very recently. What is the first thing that catches our attention? Mercury is in conjunction – literally "joined together" – with the Sun. This is testimony that the Sun signifies the thief.

The Sun signifies the thief, so in order to know if he will come back we need to find out if there is an applying aspect between the Sun and Venus, which signifies the querent. The Sun will not make any aspect with Venus. No aspect: no contact. So the querent can be assured that the thief will not return.

And so it proved. More than 4 years have passed since this question was asked. When I contacted the querent to ask permission to use this chart in this book, she confirmed that the thief has never returned.

When Will the Internet Be Cut Off?

Marcos Monteiro

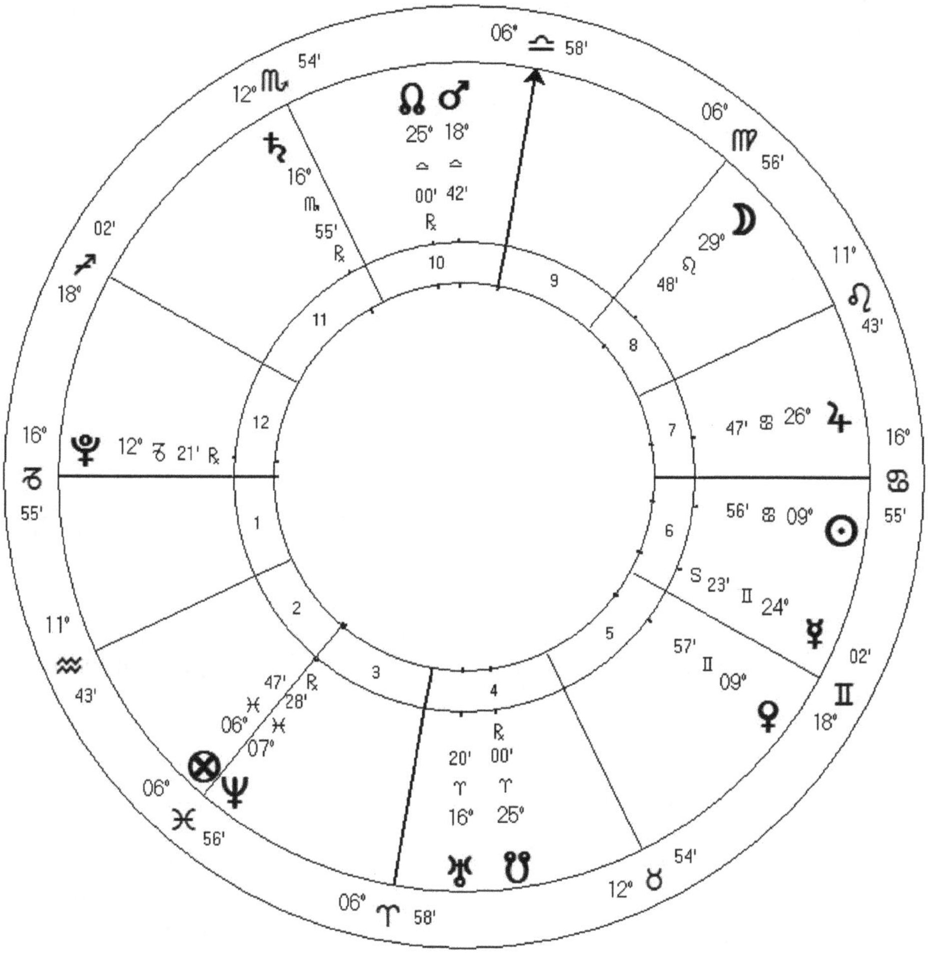

July 01, 2014, 6:01 P.M. | Barra Velha/SC, Brazil | 16 Capricorn

The querent had some unpaid internet/phone bills, for a variety of reasons. The service would be suspended at some point, and the querent wanted to know when; he would have to use an alternative until he managed to pay his debt. He stressed that he was interested in the internet connection.

The querent is Saturn, ruler of the first house. But what is the internet service?

There are two possible ways to answer this; fortunately, both point to the same planet.

In astrology, the people that do you a service – either by force, such as slaves; by a complicated social connection, such as servants; or by mutual agreement, such as employees or contracted workers – are represented by the sixth house. They are, or should be, subordinate to the person signified by the first house, the querent.

The internet service is, well, a service. So, the people who provide it are signified by the lord of the sixth, Mercury. Mercury will soon move from Gemini (its own sign, where it's very happy and is indifferent to Saturn, the querent) into Cancer (a sign in which it has no major dignity and hates Saturn).

The servants don't have to like the querent to do their job; but in this context, the change seems to represent well what is happening.

However, the ruler of the house of servants is the servants – the actual people. I was asking for the service itself. We don't have a "house of internet connection" in the sky, but we have a natural ruler of communications and information exchange, which would do the job. This ruler is also Mercury.

What does the upcoming sign change tell us about what will happen to the service? It will lose all dignity, but that's not enough; the question is not about its quality.

There is something else: Gemini's a voiced sign; Cancer, a mute one. The connection will stop talking, as it were.

Now we can say, with a certain amount of confidence, that Mercury changing sign shows the internet service being cut off. This will happen in 5 degrees and a half, so it will be cut in five units and a half. Which unit should we use?

The question was asked at the end of the day; it was unlikely that the service would be disconnected after 6 P.M. So "minutes" was not an option. Months would not make sense. Hours, days, and weeks would be a good theoretical framework.

In fact, however, our results exclude the extremes. Five and a half hours would imply that the telephone company would cut the service at 11:30 P.M.; weeks would mean they would maintain it for more than a month.

So, we have five and a half days. Since Mercury was in station, about to start moving again, I thought that maybe it could happen a bit later: my judgment was "between five and seven days".

On Monday, July the 7th, at 6:00 A.M., five days and a half after the chart was cast, the internet connection was suspended.

Will Scotland Leave the UK?

Fotini Christodoulou

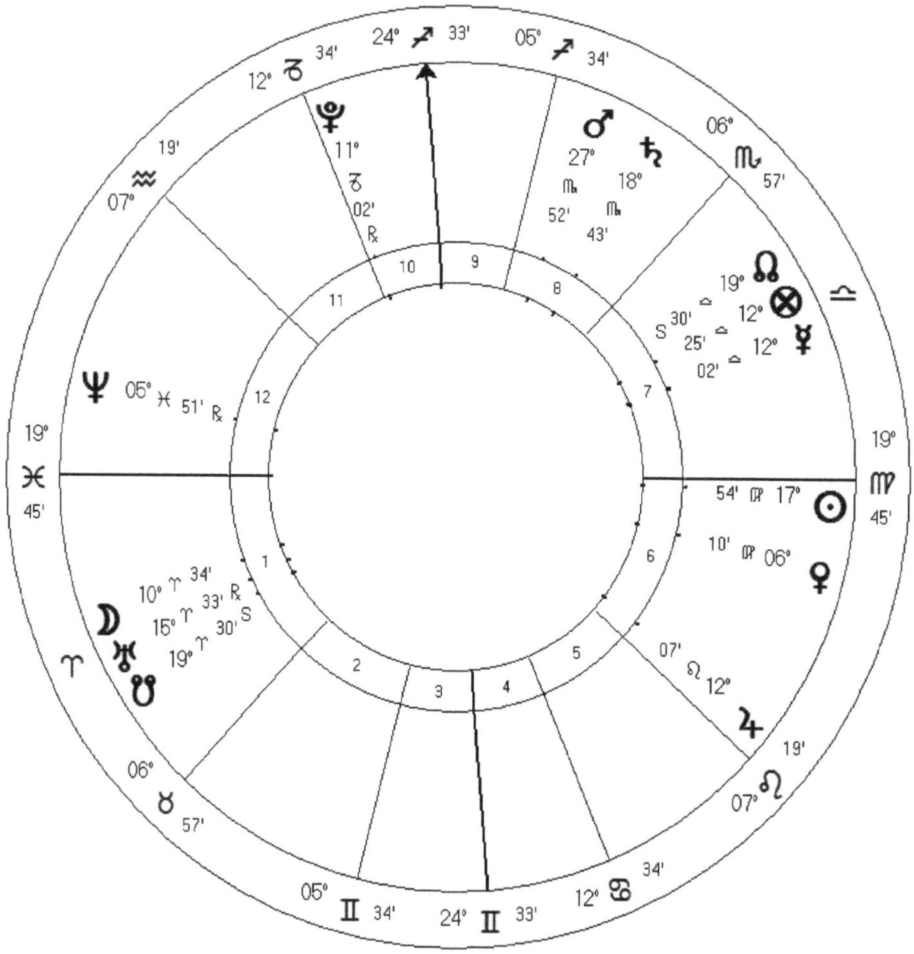

September 10, 2014, 7:46 P.M. | Thessaloniki, Greece | 19 Pisces

Scotland is a foreign country to the querent, therefore it is signified by the radical 9th and its lord. One would argue that Scotland is already a part of UK and so it is: but the question demands to differentiate Scotland from its UK partners, as it is voting for its independence.

Therefore Scotland is signified by Lord 9, Jupiter. The UK as its partner is the radical 3rd (7th from the 9th), and its lord is Mercury. In this case we would look for oppositions or a change of the significator that could suggest their leaving. But there is nothing to suggest such a change in this chart. And of course we'd have to look for the common people, the voters, shown by the Moon. Theoretically we'd look for the Moon's next aspect to judge what would be the result of the voting. But in this chart before the Moon is able to form its next aspect to Jupiter, Mercury – the UK, the partner – catches Jupiter first, perfecting their immediate sextile. In the context, this can only mean that their partnership is renewed. Scotland stays with the UK.

The Kidnapped Priest

John Frawley

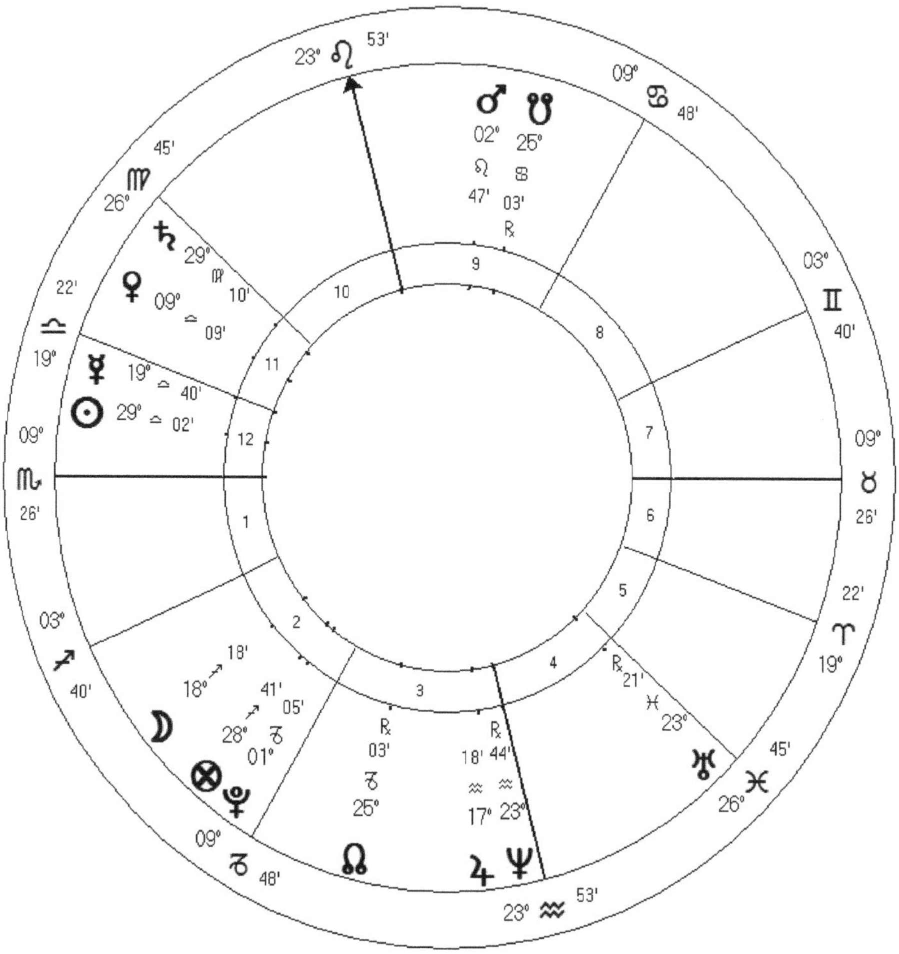

October 22, 2009, 8:42 A.M. | London, England | 9 Scorpio

"My mother's cousin is a priest, who's been doing wonderful humanitarian work in a remote area of (country). He's been kidnapped by separatist guerrillas. He's an old man, recovering from major heart surgery, and doesn't have his medication with him. Will he survive? How is he being treated? Will he be released, and if so, when?"

Had the querent asked about "that nice Father Jimmy who came to our parish once…" we would have taken his significator as Lord 9, because she is asking about a priest. But the querent is asking about him as a relative, who happens to be a priest, so we must identify him as a relative.

Cousins, like brothers and sisters, are 3rd house. He is the mother's cousin, so is shown by the 3rd house from the 10th, which is the 12th of the radical chart. This is ruled by Venus, which therefore signifies him.

Venus is in the turned 12th house (the 12th from his own house), which is congruent with him being a captive. But this is irrelevant: we know he is a captive and he would be just as much so were Venus not in the turned 12th. Venus has lots of dignity, being in its own sign. In some contexts we could read this as showing that he is happy, but this is unlikely in these circumstances. We could read it as confirming that he is one of the good guys, as the querent tells us, but this too has no relevance to the question.

The first step is to find out if he will die. If he will not die as a captive, he must sooner or later be released: there is no other option. Death will be shown by an aspect between Venus and the ruler of either the turned or radical 8th house. The ruler of the turned 8th house (8th from the 12th is the radical 7th) is also Venus. Venus cannot aspect itself, so there is no death shown there. The radical 8th is ruled by Mercury. There is no applying aspect between Venus and Mercury, showing that he will die, nor a separating aspect showing that he is dead already. With no aspect connecting him to death, he must live, and so must be released.

The Moon has aspected Venus and now makes an immediate aspect to Mercury. This would be a translation of light connecting the priest to death. But the aspect to Venus is not the most recent the Moon has made. Its last aspect was to Jupiter, so it is not translating light from Venus to Mercury.

Mercury's placement so close to the cusp of the priest's house is not testimony of death. This shows us only the querent's concern in the matter: she is worried that he may die.

Had the querent asked about her own death, finding the same planet signifying both her and death would not allow us to judge that she will not die. In that case we would have to find an alternative significator for either her or death. In this chart we don't need to do this because we already have an alternative significator for death: Mercury, ruler of the radical 8th.

There is no reason to consider the state of the priest's health. We are not concerned with that, but only with the Yes or No of whether he will die. Nor, if he were to die, would that necessarily be connected with the state of his health.

To find out how he is being treated we must identify the people who are doing the treating: the kidnappers. First choice would be the ruler of the priest's 12th house, his own house of captivity. That is Mercury. The chart shows us clearly that this cannot signify the kidnappers. It is not only ruled by Venus but is placed immediately inside the priest's house. It is completely in his power. This would be fine if he had kidnapped them, but does not fit with them kidnapping him.

The next choice would be the ruler of the radical 12th house. But we are already using that house and its ruler to signify the priest. A planet can play more than one role in a chart, but it cannot signify the two leading players if they need to interact with each other. That would be like having the same actor playing both Romeo and Juliet.

We cannot use the ruler of the priest's 7th house, showing his open enemies, because the kidnappers are not his open enemies. They haven't kidnapped him because they don't like him, nor do we know that they are mistreating him in any way.

We must work from what we know. The one thing we know for certain about his situation with regard to the kidnappers is that he is in their power. Who has power over Venus? Venus is ruled by Venus, but that's no good: he hasn't kidnapped himself. It exalts Saturn. This gives Saturn a lot of power over it, and the idea of exaggeration that exaltation carries fits perfectly with the exaggerated kind of power we are talking about here. Saturn is in Virgo, the fall of Venus, so it brings Venus down. This is entirely congruent with the situation.

At the moment Saturn is in the fall of Venus, but it is on the point of changing sign. When it does this it will, like Venus itself, have lots of dignity and will be in strong mutual reception with Venus. The present state of taking Venus into its fall is sufficiently explained by the act of kidnapping him. The improvement after Saturn has changed sign shows them treating him well. On his release he confirmed that he had been treated as well as the circumstances allowed.

Venus is heading towards the cusp of its own house. A planet entering its own house will often show literally that: the person coming home. This cannot be so here, though, because when Venus reaches its own house it is still in Libra, still in the power of Saturn. If he were being released on parole or into house arrest this could fit, but that will not happen here. The only thing that can show him being released is Venus leaving the power of Saturn.

Venus leaves Libra in 21 degrees, so the priest will be freed in 21 time-units. Which units? Venus is in a cardinal sign and a succedent house. Cardinal signs show the fastest unit, succedent houses the middle unit. This combination is not the fastest (fast + fast) nor the slowest (slow + slow), so it must be the middle unit. It is possible that our choice of time-unit is between hours, days, and weeks. Or it could be between days, weeks and months. When deciding which, consider the maximum time each unit could show, if the movement in the chart were the maximum usually possible, which is 30 degrees. A release within 30 hours would be possible. A longest unit of 30 months would seem much less likely: within 30 months our elderly, ailing priest would probably be dead, or the kidnappers would have grown weary of looking after him and released him. A choice of hours, days or weeks will probably cover it – but I don't think we can be certain. My judgement was "probably 21 days, but if not that, 21 weeks". He was released in 21 days.

On leaving Libra Venus enters Scorpio, the sign of its detriment. There is no significance in this. It does not show that immediately on his release the priest's condition deteriorated or he became a bad person. All that concerns us is that he is no longer in the power of the kidnappers, as shown by Venus leaving Libra. In the instant that this happens the credits roll and the movie is over.

Glossary

Affliction
Harm being done by one planet to another.

Air
One of four elements that describe certain qualities of the zodiac signs. The air signs are hot and moist.

Angles
Cusps of the 1st, 4th, 7th, and 10th houses, known as the Ascendant, Imum Coeli, Descendant, and Midheaven respectively.

Angular
A planet in one of the angular houses (1st, 4th, 7th or 10th) is considered to be angular.

Antiscion (pl. antiscia)
The mirror image or, literally, "shadow" of a planet. A planet's antiscion is the same number of degrees from the solstitial axis (0 Cancer/0 Capricorn) on one side as the planet's bodily position is on the other. A planet's antiscion is an alternate placement of that planet in the chart.

Applying
Aspects that have not yet perfected.

Aquarius
The eleventh sign of the zodiac, ruled by Saturn.

Arabic/Arabian Parts or Lots
Points in a horoscope calculated by adding together two planets or points in the chart and subtracting a third from their sum. For example, the formula for Part of Marriage is Ascendant + Descendant - Venus.

Aries
The first sign of the zodiac, ruled by Mars.

Ascendant (aka Rising Sign; abbr. Asc)
The cusp of the 1st house. The Ascendant is the easternmost point in the chart and is found on the left.

Aspect
An angle that two planets or points in a horoscope make to each other. Aspect means "to glance at" (Latin). The aspects used in horary astrology are sextile (60 degrees), square (90 degrees), trine (120 degrees), and opposition (180 degrees).

Astrology
The study of celestial bodies and their movements, and the meaning these have in human lives and earthly events.

Barren
A planet in Gemini, Leo, or Virgo is considered to be barren, if having or not having fertility is relevant to the matter of the question.

Behold
Planets are said to behold each other when they are in signs between which an aspect is possible.

Benefic (adj.)
Positive or helpful.

Cancer
The fourth sign of the zodiac, ruled by the Moon.

Capricorn
The tenth sign of the zodiac, ruled by Saturn.

Cardinal
One of three modes (along with fixed and mutable) used to describe certain characteristics of zodiac signs. In horary, cardinal signs show action that is quick but doesn't last.

Cazimi
A planet within 17 minutes of arc of the Sun, in the same sign as the Sun, is cazimi or "in the heart of the Sun".

Chart
A commonly used term for a horoscope.

Collection of light
A process by which two planets are joined together by a third, slower planet. The two faster-moving planets both apply to aspect the third, which collects their light, thereby perfecting the aspect between them.

Combustion
Condition of a planet when it falls within 8 degrees of the Sun on either side, varying in intensity depending upon whether the planet applies to the Sun or separates from it. Combustion is the worst accidental debility a planet can have.

Conjunction
Strictly, two planets in exactly the same degree and minute of arc. More loosely, planets within two or three degrees of each other, provided that they are in the same sign.

Cosignificator
A second planet (usually the Moon) representing a person or matter in a horary chart.

Cusp
The point marking the beginning of a house in the chart. Planets outside that house, but within around five degrees of its cusp, are considered to be in that house, provided they are in the same sign as that cusp.

Degree (of celestial longitude)
The measurement of celestial longitude within the zodiac. Each of the 12 signs contains 30 degrees.

Debility (adj., debilitated)
Weakened condition of a planet. Essential debility involves sign placement; accidental dignity involves house placement and a planet's relationship to other planets in the chart.

Descendant (abbr. Dsc)
The cusp of the 7th house, opposite the Ascendant. The Descendant is the westernmost point in the chart and is found on the right.

Detriment
A planet in the sign opposite one of its own signs is in its detriment. For example, Mars is in detriment in Libra, opposite Aries which it rules. Detriment is a strong essential debility.

Dignity
A positive condition or quality of a planet. Essential dignity involves sign placement; accidental dignity involves house placement and a planet's relationship to other planets in the chart.

Dispositor
The planet that rules the sign another planet is in; for example, Mars is dispositor of Moon in Aries. We can also say, the Moon disposes to Mars or the Moon is disposited by Mars.

Double-bodied
Another term for the mutable signs of the zodiac, emphasizing the duality that is an important part of their nature.

Earth
One of four elements that describe certain qualities of the zodiac signs. The earth signs are cold and dry.

Exaltation
A strong essential dignity, second only to sign rulership. Saturn is exalted in Libra, Jupiter in Cancer, Mars in Capricorn, the Sun in Aries, Venus in Pisces, Mercury in Virgo, and the Moon in Taurus.

Face
The most minor of essential dignities a planet can have.

Fall
A planet in the sign opposite the sign of its exaltation is in its fall. Fall is an essential debility, though not as bad as detriment.

Fire
One of four elements that describe certain qualities of the zodiac signs. The fire signs are hot and dry.

Fixed
One of three modes (along with cardinal and mutable) used to describe certain characteristics of zodiac signs. In horary, fixed signs show action that is slow and stable.

Fixed star
Stars that appear to remain in a constant position of celestial longitude, in contrast to the "wandering" stars, which are the planets in our solar system. The fixed stars are seldom important in horary astrology.

Gemini
The third sign of the zodiac, ruled by Mercury.

Horary
Literally, "of the hour." The branch of astrology that provides specific answers to specific questions by means of a horoscope.

Horary Textbook, The
The Horary Textbook by John Frawley (2005, Apprentice Books) and *The Horary Textbook, Revised Edition* by John Frawley (2014, Apprentice Books). The definitive textbook on Horary Astrology and a major source of information for most of our authors. In the Revised Edition Mr. Frawley brings what he has learned in the intervening years of teaching and practice to clarify, expand upon, and correct the original text.

Horoscope
A diagram of the heavens showing the position of planets within the zodiac, and in the sky relative to a place on Earth. More commonly called a chart.

House
One of the twelve sections within a chart. There are many systems for dividing the chart into houses; in horary we use Regiomontanus.

Imum Coeli (IC)
The northernmost point of the chart and cusp of the 4th house. It is found at the bottom of the chart.

Jupiter
One of the seven celestial bodies used in traditional astrology; second after Saturn in the order of planetary spheres.

Judgment
The process of determining the answer to a horary question; also the answer itself.

Leo
The fifth sign of the zodiac, ruled by the Sun.

Libra
The seventh sign of the zodiac, ruled by Venus.

Lilly, William (1602-1681)
English astrologer, considered one of the greatest astrologers of the English-speaking world. Author of *Christian Astrology* (1647), a seminal work that remains important today.

Longitude, celestial
Measurements of a planet is in the sky relative to the vernal equinox (0 Aries), telling us where on the ecliptic it is.

Lord
The traditional term for the ruler of a house. For example, the ruler of the 4th house is Lord of the fourth or Lord 4.

Luminary
The Sun and the Moon in astrology, although for convenience we call them planets.

Malefic
Negative or harmful.

Medium Coeli (MC)
The southernmost point in a chart and cusp of the 10th house. It is found at the top of the chart.

Mercury
One of the seven celestial bodies used in traditional astrology; second to last in the order of planetary spheres, after Venus and before the Moon.

Minutes
The units of measurement within a degree. Each degree contains sixty minutes.

Moon
A luminary, one of the seven celestial bodies used in traditional astrology and last in the order of planetary spheres, after Mercury.

Mutable
One of three modes (along with cardinal and fixed) used to describe certain characteristics of zodiac signs. In horary, mutable signs show action that comes and goes.

Mute
A planet in one of the water signs (Cancer, Scorpio, or Pisces) is considered to be mute, if having or not having a voice is relevant to the matter of the question.

Neptune
An outer planet in our solar system, treated in similar fashion to the fixed stars in traditional astrology.

Nodes of the Moon
The two points where the orbit of the Moon crosses the ecliptic, which is the orbit of the Sun. The ascending node is called the North Node; the descending node is called the South Node.

Opposition
Planets 180 degrees apart (within a few degrees) are in opposition.

Outer planets
A term used to describe the three planets Uranus, Neptune, and Pluto located beyond Saturn in our solar system.

Part of Marriage (POM)
An Arabic Part used in relationship horaries to determine the significator of the relationship itself.

Peregrine
Condition in which a planet is not in any of its own dignities, nor in its detriment or fall.

Perfect (v.)
When two planets applying to aspect reach exactitude (for example, Moon arriving at 2:29 Aries perfects a square with the Sun at 2:29 Cancer).

Pisces
The twelfth sign of the zodiac, ruled by Jupiter.

Placement
A term used to describe a planet's location in the chart, either by house or by sign.

Planet
One of the seven celestial bodies in our solar system.

Pluto
An outer planet in our solar system, treated in similar fashion to the fixed stars in traditional astrology.

Prohibition
When a third planet gets in the way of two planets joining by aspect.

Querent
The person asking the question in horary astrology.

Quesited
The person or thing being asked about in horary astrology.

Rays
Light streaming from the Sun. The other celestial bodies are also said to have rays, but the term is rarely used in this sense.

Reception
The attitudes planets, and therefore whatever those planets signify, have towards each other based upon the signs they are in. Reception can be mixed or mutual. Mixed reception is when one planet has affinity for a second but the second either has no affinity for it or is antagonistic to it. Mutual reception is when two planets share the same or similar attitudes towards each other, either positive or negative.

Retrograde
The apparent backward motion of a planet from our perspective on Earth.

Rising Sign
An alternate term for Ascendant (Asc).

Ruler (or rulership)
Each sign is seen as belonging to one or other of the planets, which rules it. For example, Aries belongs to Mars, which is its ruler.

Sagittarius
The ninth sign of the zodiac, ruled by Jupiter.

Saturn
One of the seven celestial bodies used in traditional astrology; first in the order of planetary spheres, below the sphere of the fixed stars.

Saunders, Richard (1613-1692)
English astrologer, author of *The Astrological Judgement and Practice of Physick* (1677). The diagnostic section is astonishingly accurate, his lists of typical symptoms often giving the exact words that clients will use to describe the problem.

Scorpio
The eighth sign of the zodiac, ruled by Mars.

Separating
Aspects that have already perfected.

Sextile
Planets 60 degrees apart (within a few degrees) are in sextile.

Sign
A section of the zodiac containing 30 degrees of celestial longitude. The signs, in order, are Aries, Taurus, Gemini, Cancer, Leo, Virgo, Libra, Scorpio, Sagittarius, Capricorn, Aquarius, and Pisces.

Significator (or signifier)
The planet that signifies the inquiring person (querent) or the matter asked about (quesited).

Square
Planets 90 degrees apart (within a few degrees) are in square.

Station
Not moving. Planets are in station just before going retrograde, and just before going direct again after having been retrograde.

Sun
A luminary, one of the seven celestial bodies used in traditional astrology and fourth in order of the planetary spheres, after Mars and before Venus.

Succedent
The 2nd, 5th, 8th, and 11th houses of the chart, which follow the angular houses (to succeed meaning to follow, in Latin).

Taurus
The second sign of the zodiac, ruled by Venus.

Term
A minor essential dignity, less than triplicity but greater than face.

Testimony
Evidence in a horary chart used to determine the answer to the question asked.

Translation of light
A planet making an aspect to one planet and then to a second planet is said to translate, or carry, the light of the first planet aspected to the second one. It thus connects those two planets, as if those planets themselves were making an aspect.

Trine
Planets 120 degrees apart (within a few degrees) are in trine.

Triplicity
An essential dignity, less than rulership or exaltation but greater than term or face.

Turned
A term used to identify a planet or house whose meaning is derived from other houses.

Turning the chart
Deriving one house from another is called turning the chart. For example, the querent's possessions are shown by the 2nd house. But if the question is about the querent's child's possessions we must turn the chart to look at the child's 2nd house.

Uranus
An outer planet in our solar system, treated in similar fashion to the fixed stars in traditional astrology.

Venus
One of the seven celestial bodies used in traditional astrology; fifth in the order of planetary spheres, after the Sun and before Mercury.

Via combusta
Area of the zodiac between 15 Libra and 15 Scorpio where the Moon is especially debilitated. It means "the burned-up road."

Virgo
The sixth sign of the zodiac, ruled by Mercury.

Void of course
A condition of the Moon after it has made its last aspect in one sign, before it enters the next sign. This can also be said of any planet that must travel many degrees before making its next aspect.

Water
One of four elements that describe certain qualities of the zodiac signs. The water signs are cold and moist.

Zodiac
The division of the ecliptic into twelve sections known as signs, based on the seasons, starting at 0 Aries which marks the spring equinox.

Index

Author Index

Author Biographies

Fotini Christodoulou is a full-time practitioner and teacher of traditional astrology.

She has been actively involved with astrology for the past 10 years, working as a columnist for a popular Greek website and magazines, hosting radio shows on astrological issues, writing for astrological magazines and frequently giving lectures at astrological events.

Fotini is a graduate of both John Frawley's Horary Apprenticeship, with a diploma as Horary Craftsman, and of the Natal Apprenticeship, with a diploma as Craftsman Astrologer.

Contact: horarycraftsman@gmail.com

Leah Cuperman became interested and started learning astrology at a young age. She studied Horary Astrology under John Frawley's tuition, and in 2012 graduated with a Horary Craftsman diploma. She has been practicing horary, answering questions for clients from different countries and cultures, and has collected a wide variety of charts on varied subjects that have proved to be correct.

While keeping her practice, she is also studying Natal Astrology under John's tuition.

She is available to answer Horary questions. Details on consultations, type of questions that can be judged, chart examples and contact details can be found at www.leahcuperman.com

John Frawley has been a full-time teacher and practitioner of traditional astrology since 1994, with clients and students around the world. He is author of *The Real Astrology* (Spica Award: International Book of the Year); *The Real Astrology Applied*; *The Horary Textbook*; and *Sports Astrology*

Marcos Vinicius Monteiro is a Brazilian astrologer and translator. Among his works are the Portuguese translations of John Frawley's *The*

Horary Textbook and Anthony Griffin's *Astrological Judgment of Theft*. He also teaches two courses, an *Introduction to Astrological Symbolism* and a course on Horary Astrology, and sees clients. He can be found at: .

Molly Morrissey is a decision-making, communications, and resilience expert who uses traditional astrology as a tool to provide seasoned leaders with a pragmatic framework for incorporating their emotions, intuition, and gut instinct into their intellectual, logic-based decision making process. Her work helps the client find a deeper sense of understanding about themselves and their life patterns by unearthing and connecting internal and external clues. She helps her clients build personal resilience and a realistic strategy for moving forward.

With a Master's degree in Applied Behavioral Science from Bastyr University and astrological training with master astrologer John Frawley, Molly also incorporates backgrounds in architecture and the marine industry into her unique offerings. She lives in Taos, New Mexico, USA. You can find out more or reach her at mollymorrissey.com.

Kathryn Silvestre is a practicing astrologer based in Milwaukee, Wisconsin, with students and clients from the U.S. and around the world. She studied under John Frawley, earning both his Horary Craftsman and Craftsman Astrologer diplomas. Kathryn teaches horary as she was taught, one-to-one with students via email correspondence. She loves writing about astrology on her blog, The Sun's Joy, which is published on her website. For more information please visit: www.kathrynsilvestre.com.

Lightning Source UK Ltd.
Milton Keynes UK
UKHW031452160821
388947UK00009B/1926